Jocky's Journey

by Peter Caproni and Norrie Price

Published by Norrie Price

First published in Great Britain 2013

© 2013 Norrie Price

British Library Cataloguing in Publication Data.

A catalogue record for this book is available from the
British Library.

ISBN - 978-0-9521426-5-2

Printed by Winter and Simpson Print, Dundee
Telephone 01382 813813
Typesetting and Origination by N Price

Contents

Acknowledgements

I**n writing** this book many hours were spent researching details of Jocky Scott's football career at all the clubs he was involved as a player, coach and manager. Our thanks to Jocky for his time, assistance and patience as this publication progressed. Without him there would be no book!

Many of the images used came from his own personal collection and we would like to convey our thanks to DC Thomson & Co Ltd, (Dundee), in particular Barbara Briggs, for allowing us to reproduce photographs from Jocky's career. Likewise, thanks to Dave Martin (Fotopress), and David Young, (David Young Photography), for their fine selection of images. Indeed, Fotopress should be applauded for their contribution to the visual side of football in the city of Dundee over a 40-year period, for it has been immense.

SNS Group, (Amanda Murray), too, along with Scotsman Publications, (Kerry Black) and Aberdeen Journals, (Kirsty Shand), came up with some splendid material while football afficionados such as Gordon Gurvan, Mark Robertson, Stephen Borland, Alan Wilson, (DCT), Len Smith, (Repro Overflow), Malcolm Panton, (Historic Aberdeen), Dave Johnston, (Aberdeen FC), Laura Watt and Ian Lumsden also kindly provided images, information or were there to provide a helping hand when needed.

Photographs have been acknowledged where known but while every effort has been made to trace the ownership of images and illustrations used, apologies are given should copyright inadvertantly have been infringed.

Thanks, too, to Kenny Ross for his encouragement and to him and Jacqui Robertson for permission to use an excerpt from their book *It's All About the Memories*. Reference was also made to Jim Hendry's *Dundee Greats, Aberdeen: A Centenary History* by Kevin Stirling, and the *Aberdeen Football Companion* by Clive Leatherdale. No doubt our wives will be relieved that once again they can have our undivided attention! Thanks for all your patience and thanks too to other family members who also played their part.

Top marks to Jimi Sutherland for his excellent cover design and to Derek Souter of DJS Creative Marketing for facilitating this. And our grateful thanks to Ken Winter, Steve Simpson, Alan Brown and Dave Smith in particular at Winter and Simpson Print who eased the burden as the project neared completion. Last but not least, we would like to express our gratitude to Craig Brown, (OBE), the former Scotland international team manager, a man who has associations with both Dundee and Aberdeen Football Clubs, who kindly agreed to write the foreword.

Introduction

S ome three years ago, while Jocky Scott was in his third spell as Dundee FC manager, Peter Caproni saw the merits of writing the story of his career. Thus began something of a marathon with the almost inevitable spells of turbulence before finally reaching the clear waters beyond. Peter then was the originator before being joined by Scottish Football Historian Norrie Price, who initially came on board as editor and contributor, ultimately assuming the role of publisher of a story that simply had to be told.

Peter, who himself had many years in the game, had this to say: "I first met Jocky Scott while on trial and training full-time at Dens Park in 1965. Later I had the privilege of playing against him when I joined Stirling Albion and we met again whilst Jocky was manager of Scotland's Under-16 squad and I was acting physio."

"He was a player of great pace, skill and imagination. Some would describe him as mercurial, moody even. But when he turned it on - as he did much of the time - then it was all to the benefit of his team as well as the supporters, who certainly appreciated his dashing style and the excitement he brought to the game."

"Jocky was a star for both Dundee and Aberdeen and represented Scotland at full international level. He won a League Cup winner's medal with each of his teams, memorably scoring a semi-final hat-trick for the Dons in their 5-1 triumph over Rangers in 1976. In all, Jocky made a total of over 500 appearances for both clubs and was well worth his weight in goals in a memorable playing career."

"On hanging up his boots, Scott went on to manage Dundee three times, enjoyed a successful spell as co-manager at Aberdeen and had a varied coaching and managerial career north and south of the border as well as on mainland Europe. Thus, having played and managed at both North-East clubs, the name of Jocky Scott is indelibly written into the fabric of their history books. There was failure as well as success but Jocky's lengthy career was never less than fascinating and, just as it was an honour for me to share the same pitch, it is now the privilege of Norrie and myself to present this account of his experiences in *Jocky's Journey*."

Foreword

by

CRAIG BROWN (CBE)

I **am privileged** to have known and admired Jocky Scott for almost five decades. In 1964, a shy young lad arrived at Dens Park from Chelsea to begin a hugely successful love affair with Dundee Football Club. I had been there during the halcyon days of the early sixties and playing alongside him in reserve games I could see just how talented a footballer he was. Some nine months later, I moved on but the best was still to come from Jocky Scott.

After excelling as a player, Jocky graduated to management and to supplement his knowledge he became a regular at the various SFA coaching courses. On the training field too it soon became obvious that he had the ability to go far and on looking at the variety of coaching and managerial roles he undertook in his long and distinguished career, it is quite clear that he managed to realise that early potential.

Indeed, when new Sunderland manager Howard Wikinson called to ask if I could recommend a coach, I had no hesitation in nominating Jocky with Howard phoning me back a few days later to say how well Jocky had performed. More recently, whilst managing Motherwell in 2010, I asked Jocky to visit Iceland to provide scouting reports on our UEFA Cup opponents Bredablick - needless to say, his findings helped us win the tie.

Thus, I'm pleased to say that my early assessment of his coaching abilities proved quite correct, his success in club management thoroughly vindicating my judgement. Jocky Scott was rightly inducted to the Dundee FC Hall of Fame and were there to be a Hall of Fame for Scottish Football coaches, he would be one of the outstanding candidates for inclusion. Indeed there would be no more deserving recipient among the football fraternity for being a thorough gentleman than Jocky Scott esquire.

Chapter 1

Granite City

John Alexander Scott was born in Aberdeen on January 14th, 1948. Clement Attlee was Prime Minister and Great Britain was still recovering from the aftermath of the Second World War. That year had also seen the birth of the National Health Service in a society weary but disciplined by war and accustomed to austerity. People who had become used to little were content with simple things. Cinema, sport and radio combined with "holidays at home" or the British seaside and Butlin's camps provided the entertainment, there being little travel abroad.

Ration books were the order of the day, women, mostly, were housewives and men were the breadwinners. In those days, the game of football was part and parcel of everyday life for it was accepted that the men of the house went to football on Saturdays and attendances of that era were certainly testimony to that. In the post-war years almost every senior club experienced bumper gates, with Aberdeen and Dundee, the clubs with whom John Scott - only later was it Jocky - would be most closely associated, both enjoying considerable success as well as average home attendances stretching to well over 20,000.

Between 1946 and 1965, the Old Firm faced fierce competition from provincial clubs like Hibs, Dundee, Aberdeen and Hearts who challenged strongly while various others like Motherwell, East Fife, Falkirk, St Mirren, Dunfermline and Kilmarnock also enjoyed moments of glory. In season 1946-47, Aberdeen won the Scottish Cup by defeating Hibs, having earlier lost to Rangers in the League Cup Final.

In '48/49, Dundee were pipped for the Scottish League Championship by a single point, but went on to win the League Cup in 1951 against Rangers and in 1952 against Kilmarnock, just failing to notch a hat-trick of Hampden triumphs by losing to Motherwell in the Scottish Cup Final before a quite remarkable crowd of 136,274 in April 1952.

The following season, the Dons lost to Rangers in the Scottish Cup Final, but in season 1954-55, with the young Scott just six and a half years old, Aberdeen won the biggest prize of all - the Scottish League Championship. In those days, youngsters tended to support their local club and as a keen Dons fan, he began to watch and learn from his heroes who wore the red and white of Aberdeen.

It was a successful period for the Dons and just a few months after winning the league, Aberdeen added the League Cup by defeating St Mirren and only narrowly failed to retain the championship. So it was, then, that John Scott

9

and his little friends enjoyed replaying the Dons' famous victories on their own personal "pitch" on the street outside his home in Urquhart Road, only minutes away from Pittodrie.

His father, Willie Scott - nicknamed "Bunty" - had played centre-forward for Aberdeen between 1935 and 1938, scoring eight goals in 38 appearances before signing for Newcastle United. There, he netted twice in nine first-team games before the advent of the Second World War brought a premature end to his football career. Scott senior joined the British Army but was captured just four months after the German invasion of France in May 1940. He was to spend the rest of the war in a Prisoner of War Camp and, like many others, the best years of his career had gone.

Accordingly, the youngster got sound advice from his father but otherwise there was no coaching as we know it back in the 1950s. Instead, he would practice for hours on end, knocking the ball against the uneven wall, where it could rebound unexpectedly and awkwardly, and it was there that Scott honed his skills, developing his touch and ball control. And so against this background, it was perhaps no surprise that Scott would go on to become a professional footballer.

Soon the Scott family moved to Kincorth Place in the Kincorth area of Aberdeen and it was at Abbotswell Primary School that Scott first played competitive football. Soon his predatory goal-scoring talent was evident and he became a key figure as the school proceeded to win several local cup competitions with the finals played at Aberdeen FC's Pittodrie Park.

The young Aberdonian's Dons' heroes were Graham Leggat and Jackie Hather, who were both wingers, the position initially favoured by Scott, who began as an old-fashioned outside-right. The speedy Leggat, a Scottish inter-nationalist, was at Pittodrie for five seasons knocking in 64 goals in 109 matches for Aberdeen before joining Fulham for £16,000, a considerable fee at that time. Leggat was equally comfortable playing through the middle, and so in time it would prove with Scott.

Later, it was yet another Aberdonian, Denis Law, who would command Scott's adulation. Law had burst to prominence with Huddersfield before joining Manchester City for a British record fee of £55,000 in 1960. A year later, he went to Torino before returning to sign for Manchester United, where he spent the bulk of his career. The lightning-quick Law was arguably Scotland's greatest ever internationalist with 55 caps and Scott, similar in style, made no secret of his admiration, even adopting the Law habit of grasping his jersey sleeve cuffs which would be recognised as one of his own trademarks in years to come!

In 1960, Scott graduated to Aberdeen Grammar School, but despite doing well at maths and woodwork, he was singularly focussed on becoming a professional footballer. Scott's talent was abundantly clear and in 1963 the pacy winger, who even now can recall the excitement of progressing through the highly-competitive trials, was chosen to represent the Scottish School-boys Under-16s against Ireland at St Mirren's ground in Love Street, Paisley. The Scots won with Scott doing well enough to retain his place and going on to score, unusually for him, with a header against Wales in a 2-2 draw before a bumper crowd at Ibrox.

John Scott was now mixing with schoolboy internationals, who, like himself, were destined to become household names in the future. Centre-half Arthur Thomson would prove a stalwart for Hearts, while the fabulously talented left-winger Eddie Gray went on to star for Leeds United and Scotland. In the final match at Nottingham Forest's City Ground, the Scots lost to a strong English side. But Scott had stood out, holding his own against far bigger opponents, and soon the scouts were buzzing around, clamouring for his signature!

He had no lack of choice - Aberdeen, Aston Villa, Leeds United, Preston North End and Sheffield Wednesday were all keen and soon top clubs like Rangers, Manchester United and Arsenal had also joined the race. Somewhat surprisingly, however, it was another London club, Chelsea, who had just been promoted to the English First Division, that was to succeed.

The 15-year-old Scott had been training at Pittodrie with Aberdeen for a couple of years but the early '60s were a lean time for the Dons and in any case, his father, now a corporation bus driver, felt it might be best for young John to pursue his career outwith the city. Chelsea's Scottish scout, John King, a Dundonian, visited the Scott household several times before per-suading Scott to come south to visit Stamford Bridge.

A flight in a Vickers Viscount took an excited Scott and his father to London Airport and from there a taxi took them across the capital to meet Chelsea boss Tommy Docherty, who had had an illustrious playing career with Celtic, Preston North End and Arsenal as well as making a total of 25 appearances for Scotland.

The "Doc" had ended his playing career with a handful of games while player-manager at Chelsea only to suffer relegation in 1961-62. But he had then revitalised the club, clearing out many of the older players, before lead-ing them to promotion in '62/63. Fellow Scot Docherty was a persuasive character and, highly impressed with what he had to say, the young Scott was quick to put pen to paper.

Scott settled in well at his digs with Mr and Mrs Taylor at Thornton Heath in Surrey along with two other Scots hopefuls, Jimmy Stewart from Dundee and John Boyle from Motherwell. The Chelsea youth team had their own training ground at Hendon but although he quickly adapted to full-time football and loved training and playing matches, the youngster wasn't quite so keen on some of his daily chores, such as cleaning the senior players' boots and in particular, sweeping the vast terraces that used to adorn Stamford Bridge in the 1960s! "We'd play our youth games on a Saturday morning and would only go to the stadium to watch first-team games or when we had a week's groundstaff duty when you did all these menial jobs and got to train with the first team which was quite a thrill," said Scott.

In those days, Chelsea had some wonderful players such as Peter Bonetti, future Scottish international left-back Eddie McCreadie, Barry Bridges, Bobby Tambling, Terry Venables, Ron "Chopper" Harris and the veteran Frank Blunstone. At youth level, too, future stars like the legendary Peter Osgood and John Hollins were beginning to emerge, and clearly with this quality of player it would be no easy task to make the first-team break-through. However, the young Scott had done well, finishing his first season as the youth side's joint-top scorer before packing his bags and travelling back to Scotland for the summer break.

Soon though, his world would be turned upside down. "I was still in bed when the mail came through the letterbox at our new home in Morrison Drive, Garthdee in Aberdeen. My father brought me up a letter and, having recognised the Chelsea insignia on the envelope and expecting it contained details of pre-season training, I asked him to read it out. He did and there was an ominous silence as he placed it on my bed," recalled Scott.

It contained devastating news for it was an official note releasing him from his contract at Stamford Bridge. "Obviously, I was very upset and although I suppose the Doc and the coaches down there felt I was not for them, they should have told me to my face. I still wanted a career in the game so the story was put out that I'd left Chelsea because I was homesick because we didn't want to say I'd been freed." The youngster's top-level career appeared to be over before it had properly begun but, eventually putting aside his bitter disappointment, Scott returned to his Granite City Under-17 youth team ALC Spurs determined to knuckle down and prove Chelsea wrong.

Chapter 2

The Road and the Miles

I t was 1964 and that May the Granite City experienced a serious epidemic of typhoid, a highly infectious and potentially life-threatening disease whose source was traced to a tin of South American corned beef sold from the local branch of the grocery chain, William Low. Some 500 people were affected and quarantined in hospital as the city came to a near standstill with Aberdonians discouraged from travelling outside and outsiders afraid to venture in. There were no deaths, nor, fortunately, was the Scott household affected and with the city declared safe in July, the budding young footballer got another crack at the big time.

Soon after returning to Aberdeen's public parks, John Scott was spotted by a Dundee FC scout - Bob Shankly had been tipped off - and invited to Dens Park for pre-season training. This was his big chance and the young Aberdonian was determined to shine. In those days, there were no pre-season friendlies and very few glamour games. Instead, most clubs had a public trial, a game consisting of three half-hour spells to allow the manager and fans to run the rule over the playing squad and assess the ability of any of the trialists on show.

Dundee's public trial took place on a Monday evening in late July, just before the start of the 1964-65 season. Much of the interest for the 4,000 crowd centred on the appearance of the as-yet unsigned Alan Gilzean, but it was the mystery youngster at inside-right for the "Blues" that had fans talking excitedly about his skill, direct running and shooting power. In next day's report in *The Courier*, "Don Jon" revealed that the trialist who had virtually stolen the show with two great goals was: "16-year-old Aberdonian John Scott who impressed as a strong forceful boy with a wallop in either foot."

As Scott later recalled in an interview with Tom Duthie of the *Evening Telegraph*, "It was the old-fashioned trial game which involved three mini-games. First, there were the trialists v. reserves, then reserves plus trialists v. fringe players, then finally reserves, fringe players and any trialists they thought could handle it v. the first-team. I was fortunate to get to play in all the games and did well enough to be offered a contract."

The following day, Dens boss Bob Shankly motored to the Granite City to meet Scott's parents and offer him terms. Aberdeen manager Tommy Pearson was also very keen but Dundee who had been Scottish League Champions in 1962, reached the European Cup semi-final in 1963, and the Scottish Cup Final just a few months previously, were currently one of the top clubs in Scotland, and Scott was delighted to sign for them.

However, worryingly for the Dark Blues, there were signs that their great side was starting to break up. A year earlier, Scottish international centre-half Ian Ure had been sold to Arsenal for £62,500 and prolific goal-scorer Alan Gilzean was now refusing to re-sign. Scott began the new campaign in the reserves but after a poor start in which they lost four out of their opening five games and with morale at a low ebb, Bob Shankly rang the changes for the visit of Motherwell to Dens Park in the League Cup on Wednesday, August 26th.

Out went Bert Slater, Bobby Cox, Bobby Seith, Kenny Cameron and Doug Houston and, in their places Shankly included four youngsters - goalkeeper Ally Donaldson, left-back Alex Totten, right-half John Phillips and inside-right John Scott with Hugh Robertson restored to the left-wing. Dundee, who by then had no chance of qualifying from their section, lined up: *Donaldson; Hamilton, Totten; Phillips, Ryden, Stuart; Penman, Scott, Waddell, Cousin, Robertson. Motherwell: Wyllie; Thomson, McCallum; McCann, Delaney, Murray; Coakley, Lindsay, McBride, Hunter, Weir.*

The Dens boss had hoped the changes might give his side a lift but Dundee's astonishing 6-0 win must have exceeded his wildest expectations! *The Courier* reported: "The fans were singing 'Happy days are here again' as they trooped from Dens Park last night. And who would argue with them with six great goals and some vintage football from the experimental Dundee side. The name on everyone's lips was that of the dark-haired bundle of football at inside-right who transformed the Dark Blues - John Scott. The sixteen and-a-half-year-old ex-Chelsea boy struck a game right away. He was here, there and everywhere, chasing everything, and laying on some glorious balls for the eager Dundee forwards."

Dundee remained a fine footballing side but without the power and thrust of Gilzean, they had lacked that vital edge. Now, though, the introduction of the eager-beaver Scott had provided the catalyst for a devastating return to form. There were no goals for the dynamic youngster, nor did he score in the 3-1 win at Falkirk in the final League Cup game a few days later. However, the Dens starlet had again been mightily impressive until receiving his marching orders for retaliation after being fouled by Northern Ireland internationalist Sammy Wilson. *The Courier* observed: "What a tragedy, and what a lesson for a young man who I believe will go far in the game. Scott can play all right. He and Andy Penman have already struck up a fine partnership which will bring a lot of goals for Dundee in the future.

"Apparently," the report went on, "the player was so upset that almost an hour later he could hardly speak. Still, this should be a lesson for him. He won't lose his rag on the field again in a hurry I'd imagine - no matter the provocation. And how on earth was the referee to know - certainly not by the way Scott played - that he was quite so young?" Scott's potential was clear to see - he had hit the bar at Brockville and having won a penalty against Motherwell, he earned another in a 3-1 win over Aberdeen at Dens when giant defender Doug Coutts felt obliged to pull him down and Andy Penman swept the ball home from the spot.

Now came an eagerly anticipated derby with local rivals Dundee United but, since their promotion in 1960, United had made it tough for the Dark Blues and despite Dundee's far greater profile, each side had won four, lost four and drawn four of the keenly contested meetings. And now with the men in black and white winning both of this season's League Cup ties, Dundee had the unenviable record of failing to win any of their last eight derby clashes.

Dundee players and supporters, then, were desperate for revenge and despite falling behind to a Lewis Thom strike, fine goals by Alan Cousin and Bobby Waddell had the Dark Blues in front after 51 minutes. Dundee had dominated but with six minutes remaining and the game still finely balanced, John Scott pounced to roll the ball home from close in after United keeper Sandy Davie and Jimmy Briggs collided. That made it 3-1 and, soon afterwards, the youngster sent the Dundee fans in a packed Shed end wild with delight when he deftly glanced home a near-post header from Robertson's well-flighted cross!

"Well, that was the biggest game I'd ever played in and it really was some atmosphere," said Scott. Things hadn't been going well for the club earlier but the Dundee fans were great. It was only my fourth first-team appearance so what a fantastic feeling to get these two late goals and what a noise. It's an afternoon I'll never forget!"

That capped a derby glory day for Scott though suspension meant him missing Dundee's 4-1 demolition of Rangers, their fifth successive win and a result which gave them a measure of revenge for April's last-gasp Scottish Cup Final defeat by the Ibrox men. However, the revival foundered just as quickly and although Scott returned in a 2-1 home defeat by bogy team Clyde, manager Shankly recognised that the young Aberdonian remained a raw talent and eased him back into the reserves where he could continue to learn the game without the pressures involved at first-team level.

Scott was fulsome in his praise for Bob Shankly: "Shanks signed me and gave me my first-team chance at a young age and although he was hard, you knew exactly where you were with him. 'Ye're no working hard enough', he would shout, or 'dinnae just stand there, bloody move a bit quicker'. At times he would put the fear of death in you but he knew the game inside out. He also seemed to know everything that was going on in and outside Dens Park and absolutely nothing escaped him. Once about half a dozen of us had a few drinks on a Saturday night and went to the annual Haparanda dance - "The Hap" itself, on the Arbroath Road, was a popular coffee bar with the fashionable Dundee youth of the '60s - in the city's Continental Ballroom."

"Unfortunately, Phil Tinney, who had had one drink too many, was being escorted outside by a couple of doormen and when his fellow Liverpudlian John Phillips decided to lend a helping hand by diving off the top of the stairs on to the bouncers, he was thrown out as well! That Monday, Shanks had all the players involved, including me, back in the afternoons for more training. One by one we were called in to his office to explain ourselves and, of course, we all denied that we had been drinking. None more so than John Phillips only for Shanks to retort: 'Right Phillips, if that really was the case, why you were doing an impersonation of Audie Murphy!'"

"Now Audie Murphy was a famous, all-action cowboy film star of a decade earlier but Shankly was well aware of the players' misbehaviour and his actions showed us he had his finger on the pulse. The players all respected him so much that going to see Shankly in his office was a bit like a schoolboy going in to see the headmaster. There's another great story about a young centre-half called Billy McMillan who felt his performances in the reserves merited a chance in the first team."

"Guys like Alex Hamilton were winding him up and eventually he decided to go and see the manager. Imagine the scenario - Billy nervously going in to Shankly's office with half the dressing room listening outside! Clearly the meeting wasn't going according to plan and Shanks's voice was getting louder 'I'll tell you if ye're ready to play in the team, you're no telling me.'"

"Billy, though, kept nipping away until Shankly, after threatening to chase him out the door, eventually did so and finished up pursuing the distraught player out on to the street outside Dens Park. Of course the story grew arms and legs over time with some even saying that Shanks chased Billy - he was a big lad - all the way down to Tannadice! McMillan, though, did play several first-team games and after leaving in 1962 went on to have a fine career in the educational field."

As Scott settled in, it proved a season of transition for Dundee, who by February found themselves out of the Scottish Cup - to newly promoted St Johnstone - as well as the European Cup Winners' Cup. As Shankly recast his side, familiar names such as Bert Slater, Bobby Seith, George Ryden and Bobby Waddell disappeared from the team-sheet but, more significantly, Dundee's Scotland international forward, Alan Gilzean, scorer of 169 goals in 190 competitive games, had been transferred to Tottenham Hotspur for a Scottish record fee of £72,500 after briefly returning to the side.

Increasingly disillusioned at the loss of his star players, Bob Shankly resigned and was appointed Hibernian manager in place of Jock Stein, who had moved to Celtic. Sammy Kean, took charge temporarily before the appointment of Bobby Ancell and the new Dens boss's first game on Saturday, April 3rd would be against none other than Hibernian, with Bob

Shankly making an early return to his old Dens Park stamping ground. In one of the most open league championships for many years, Hibs, as well as Hearts, Kilmarnock and Dunfermline were battling it out for the title.

Gilzean's departure had prompted the £40,000 signing of Aberdeen's Scotland Under-23 international, Charlie Cooke. And although that had caused dismay in John Scott's Granite City hometown, Cooke's brilliant play inspired Dundee to spectacular victories over Hearts, 7-1 at Tynecastle, and Kilmarnock, 4-1 at Rugby Park, with Dunfermline fortunate to salvage a 3-3 draw at East End Park. Scott, meanwhile had continued to impress in the reserves, and an injury to Kenny Cameron, saw him recalled against Bob Shankly's second-placed Hibs.

It proved a magnificent game between two of the best footballing sides in Scotland. Dundee had top quality performers like Alex Hamilton, Alan Cousin, Alex Stuart, Andy Penman, Charlie Cooke and Hugh Robertson while Hibs boasted men like Pat Stanton, Pat Quinn, Neil Martin, Peter Cormack, Eric Stevenson and the brilliant Willie Hamilton. But the vital difference between the sides was the clinical scoring ability of John Scott, who netted two well-struck goals to give Dundee a 2-1 victory in the spring sunshine. The match report in *The Sunday Post* described his finishing: "A neck or nothing clearance by Alex Hamilton landed at Andy Penman's feet. Andy glided it into Scott's path and - wham! The 'Dee were two up. A perfect pass and a perfect goal."

"It was quite incredible really. I had been on the scrapheap at Chelsea but there I was, along with Andy Penman, walking along Sandeman Street behind the main stand at Dens amongst throngs of supporters before a big game. As you headed for the players' entrance, young fans would clamour for autographs and then it was in to the dressing room, sitting amongst household names of Scottish football. Then out and down the ramp on to the pitch to the roar of 17,000 fans!"

That was virtually the end of the Easter Road challenge, while Hearts, courtesy of Dundee's Tynecastle massacre, went on to lose the championship on goal-average to Kilmarnock. The blossoming Scott, though, went on to make another two league appearances, netting another double in a 6-1 Dens win over already-relegated Third Lanark. It would be the last time the Dark Blues faced the Cathkin club who would become defunct just two years later, but there would be many more glory days for young John Scott.

Chapter 3

Learning his Trade

John Scott had done well in his first year at Dens but he had much to learn and would have to work hard to catch the eye of his new manager. Bobby Ancell, though, had a reputation for developing talented young-sters and his Fir Park youth policy had seen the emergence of stars like Bert McCann, Ian St John, Willie Hunter, Pat Quinn, John Martis and Bobby Roberts, who had been part of a fine footballing side at Motherwell. Sammy Kean had moved on to become Falkirk manager and having retired from the playing side of the game, Bobby Seith took his place as first-team coach.

"Bobby Seith was an excellent coach and I learned a lot from him but I was fortunate to have so many experienced professionals - guys like full-backs Alex Hamilton and Bobby Cox and the likes of Bobby Wishart, Alan Cousin and Hugh Robertson - to listen and learn from in my early days at Dens," said Scott. "I stayed in digs with Andy Penman and his wife Sandra and Andy had plenty of good advice for me. He, too had returned from a big English club - in his case Everton - and like me, made his Dundee debut at a very young age - just short of his 16th birthday - before playing a big part in the Championship winning side of 1961-62."

It would be late September before Scott returned to the first team. There was fierce competition for places, in Scott's case made all the harder by the £10,000 summer signing of Danish centre-forward Carl Bertelsen, who had netted 18 goals for Morton last season. "In my view Kenny Cameron was a better goalscorer than either Bertelsen or Alex Harley before him," said Scott. "Both had been prolific scorers with their previous clubs but never hit it off at Dens and Kenny saw both off until he was allowed to join Kilmarnock in 1967. I thought that was a mistake and it didn't surprise me that he continued to bang in the goals at Rugby Park and later with Dundee United."

Dundee, however, failed to qualify from their League Cup section. And although they had taken three points from Dundee United, who now featured top quality Scandinavians like Orjan Persson and Finn Dossing, the Tannadice side had stunned the Dark Blues by winning 5-0 at Dens Park in the league. That result prompted Scott's recall somewhat appropriately against Aberdeen at Pittodrie and it was to prove a memorable Granite City return as he played his part in a 3-2 victory against his boyhood heroes.

Former Dons star Charlie Cooke netted one of the goals and also involved that day was inside-forward Jim McLean, recently signed from Clyde for £10,000, and a man who was to play his part in Scott's footballing development, first as a team-mate, then as coach, before becoming a managerial adversary in later years.

It proved a rare appearance for Scott that term as Bobby Ancell sacrificed some of the flamboyance which had seen Dundee score 180 league goals in the past two seasons. However, plenty of flair remained, with the class and scoring ability of Andy Penman and the creative Charlie Cooke making them the star attractions. Cooke had his own inimitable, close-dribbling style and in a season dogged by inconsistency, his dazzling performances gave the fans something to cheer about and brought a deserved place in the Scotland international team.

Jocky has fond memories of the star quality Charlie Cooke brought to Dens Park: "I knew he was a popular player at Aberdeen but although I trained at Pittodrie, I never came across him there. Charlie was a great player with wonderful skill, two good feet, good acceleration, good to watch and great for Dundee. Sometimes, though, he was a nightmare to play with as you never knew when he was going to release the ball. As a striker you would make a run when you thought he was ready to make a pass but he would look at you sometimes then turn away and dribble."

"That would happen a couple of times and you would get fed up so the next time you thought he was going to pass you would stand still. He'd pass the ball into the space where he expected you to go but hadn't. You would look bad and obviously the fans would blame the striker for not anticipating the pass, but that said, Charlie Cooke was sheer class, a great character and really an all-round good guy."

It was around then that Scott was nicknamed "Jocky". After the morning's training, he, along with other Dens youngsters like George Stewart regularly visited a cafe in Reform Street for lunch before going on to a snooker hall at the corner of High Street: "One day there was a bit of banter and one of the lads asked if I fancied being a jocky because of my height - or lack of it! So, after that I became Jocky to all except my immediate family and now it's difficult to respond when anyone calls me by my proper name!"

Domestically, Celtic were fast emerging as the dominant force in Scottish football for Jock Stein's influence had been huge. Last term, he had led them to Scottish Cup glory against Dunfermline and when Dundee fell 2-0 to the cup holders in February 1966, the Dark Blues had little to play for. Most of the iconic names from the glory days of the early '60s had gone and Alex Hamilton, too, appeared on his way out.

The chirpy defender, who had made a Dundee FC record of 24 Scotland appearances, had recently lost his international place. And, following the untimely cup exit, his club career was also in decline after the signing of highly-rated Cowdenbeath right-back, Bobby Wilson. Soon that prompted a transfer request from the unhappy Hammy with Penman also making it clear that he wanted away.

But it was Charlie Cooke, disillusioned at Dundee's lack of progress and unsettled after mixing with highly paid Anglos on Scotland duty, who moved on, Chelsea paying £72,000 soon after he was voted Dundee FC's Player of the Year. This came as a great shock to the fans as Cooke, who had only been at Dens for 16 months, was under contract for another season. His departure, however, gave Scott his chance in the four remaining league games of '65/66. And although the struggling Dark Blues managed only a single point, it had given the young Aberdonian the opportunity to show just what he was capable of.

Cooke's transfer to Chelsea no doubt prompted thoughts of what might have been for Scott, all the more so when the Stamford Bridge side arrived at Dens Park for a pre-season friendly as part of the deal. The ex-Chelsea youth had also witnessed the visit of Arsenal, who won 7-2, in November 1964, and would see Tottenham Hotspur (3-2 winners), in 1966, in challenge matches as part of the Ure and Gilzean transfers. These glamour games attracted bumper attendances with another 15,000 crowd, no doubt stimulated by the excitement of that summer's World Cup Finals in England, turning out to see Chelsea depart with a 2-1 win.

Much of Dundee's season would again be dogged by inconsistency and although Scott played a number of League Cup games he soon slipped back into the shadows. There was a fine 4-1 derby win at Tannadice in September but Jerry Kerr's Dundee United avenged this with a 3-2 triumph in the return fixture in early January 1967 - though not before John Scott had set Dens Park alight with a penetrating run and shot which simply raged into the postage stamp corner of the net soon after kick-off!

Dundee's defensive problems persisted and cost them dear as they were routed 5-0 by a Jimmy Smith-inspired Aberdeen in the Scottish Cup at Dens. For several years, the Dons had struggled but new boss Eddie Turnbull had transformed them into a tough, tight unit that went on to reach the final where they finished runners-up to Celtic, winners of the European Cup and the Scottish domestic treble.

That defeat heralded Andy Penman's departure to Rangers with George McLean - one of the scapegoats for the Ibrox side's shock cup defeat by Berwick Rangers - coming to Dens in part-exchange athough the new man was ineligible to play having arrived after the transfer deadline. By then, Scott had become a first-team regular as had another 19-year-old, centre-half George Stewart, as Dundee hit their best form in years, losing just once in their last nine games to finish sixth, with Scott celebrating his 13th goal of the campaign in the final match, a 1-1 draw against Rangers at Dens Park.

"It was a really exciting time for me," said Scott. "That summer, we jetted off on a month-long tour of the USA and returned unbeaten after 11 games. We flew in to New York and also played at Boston, St Louis, Philadelphia, San Francisco, Los Angeles and Miami. That trip was a marvellous experience for us all. We scored 62 goals of which I got eleven though both George and Jim McLean - nicknamed "Dandy" and "Beano" - got a couple more!"

"In California, we met the great Dundee and Scotland star of the 1950s, Billy Steel, but the footballing highlights were undoubtedly the 4-2 wins over English League First Division Champions Manchester United who had the legendary Bobby Charlton, Denis Law and George Best, and FA Cup runners-up Chelsea, Ron "Chopper" Harris and all! It was a huge thrill for me to play against my boyhood hero Denis Law and when we played Chelsea in a second game in Miami, I came up against John Boyle who I'd stayed with in digs when I was at Stamford Bridge."

"There were some hilarious off-field memories as well. Our centre-half George Stewart had never been out of Scotland and when we arrived at the Sheraton Atlantic Hotel in New York - our first stop – he collected his room key and a few of us made our way up together in the lift to his floor. When we arrived there a voice from the wall of the floor said 'You are now at the tenth floor.' On leaving the lift, George, without hesitation, replied 'thank you' which sent us all into hysterics as he was deadly serious!"

"Later, Stevie Murray and I borrowed a car from someone to drive around Los Angeles which on reflection was a bit of a tall order for a couple of teenagers who had not long passed their driving tests. We devised a plan that Stevie would steer and work the pedals and I would change gears as it wasn't an automatic. Everything appeared to go well for a couple of minutes until a car approached us from the opposite direction. Only then did we realise that we were driving on the wrong side of the road!"

Chapter 4

A Regular Game

Dundee had discovered a winning formula and this continued into the 1967-68 season with Hibs, Motherwell and Clyde eliminated at the sectional stage before East Fife were crushed 5-0 on aggregate in the quarter-finals. The Dark Blues extended their unbeaten record from the season before to a remarkable 24 games before suffering their first defeat in early September. Scott though soon gave way to the more experienced George McLean who soon became a big fans favourite and went on to net a remarkable total of 35 goals that season. "I couldn't really complain as I was a bit inconsistent then. Big Dandy had a very direct style, a bit like myself. Most of the time he was a lethal finisher though he could miss some howlers," said Scott.

"Sammy Wilson, in contrast, was not so fast but great with the headed flicks and lay-offs - a good foil for the pacier guys. Jim McLean was a clever player and had begun to play that bit deeper and he and Sammy had a really good understanding. And the balance was made up with wee Billy Campbell - like Sammy, a Northern Ireland international signed for just £3,000 from Sunderland - giving us great penetration from the right wing. He was straight from the Jimmy Johnstone and Willie Henderson mould - small and pacy but with the heart of a lion. He was really popular with the fans," Scott recalled.

"I got a wee run in September and played in the quarter-final games against East Fife but by the time of the semi-final against St Johnstone in mid-October, I had dropped out of the side. But although Dundee went in at half-time a goal down, there was a terrific atmosphere at Tannadice that night and lifted by tremendous support from the terraces, the boys went on to win 3-1 and reach a cup final for the first time since 1964!"

Defeats in the next two games left manager Ancell with a selection dilemma for the Scottish League Cup Final on Saturday, October 28th. In the end, Jocky Scott was left out and had to sit in the stand along with goalkeeper Ally Donaldson with former skipper Bobby Cox named substitute as the teams lined up - *Dundee: Arrol; Wilson R, Houston; Murray, Stewart, Stuart; Campbell, McLean J, Wilson S, McLean G and Bryce. Sub. - Cox. Celtic: Simpson; Craig, Gemmell; Murdoch, McNeil, Clark; Chalmers, Lennox, Wallace, Auld, Hughes. Sub. - O'Neill.*

"There was a lot of excitement in the build up for the final, team photos being taken and interviews, although it was disappointing for me not to play, said Scott. "We had around 12,000 fans in the crowd of 66,000 that day and if we hadn't been so slow to start, might have done better. We lost two early goals and although we settled to play some great football going forward, we struggled defensively and lost 5-3. However, that was a pretty good performance against a Celtic team probably at their peak and who had just recently participated in the World Club Championship against Racing Club of Argentina."

It was December before Scott returned to the side again and by then a pattern had emerged. "We could raise our game for cup competitions but struggled in the league and although we scored plenty of goals, we often lost even more. There were some incredible scorelines such as us losing 5-4 to Celtic and 4-3 to Partick Thistle, then defeating Kilmarnock 6-5, all at Dens Park. So, the punters were getting goals galore and great value for money though it must have been tough on their nerves!" said Scott.

"We played Rangers in the Scottish Cup before huge crowds - 33,000 at Dens then 54,000 at Ibrox - but although we went out after extra-time in the replay and eventually finished ninth in the league, we still remained in the Inter-Cities Fairs Cup. It was a bit of a bonus that Dundee were involved but with only one team per city allowed and Rangers, who'd been second last term and fifth-placed Hibs already in, Clyde, who finished third had been denied entry, and despite us only being sixth, we were back in Europe!"

"When I first arrived at Dens I heard all about the great European nights so it was great to be involved as a substitute against the Dutch side DWS Amsterdam, who we beat 4-2 on aggregate. I was also on the bench for the games against Royal Liege of Belgium, who we overcame 7-2 after big George got all four in Liege. I then played in the quarter-final ties against FC Zurich both of which we won by the only goal and that set us up for a "Battle of Britain" clash with Leeds United in the semi-finals."

"European football seemed to suit us and the measured build-up of our opponents perhaps gave our defenders more time to get organised, but now we faced a powerful Leeds team who had already eliminated Rangers and Hibs. They had big names such as Billy Bremner, Jackie Charlton, Norman Hunter, Peter Lorimer and Eddie Gray and to allow us to better compete with them in midfield, Alex Kinninmonth, a clever, hard-working midfielder, got the nod ahead of me."

The first leg was at Dens before a crowd of nearly 25,000 and although the Yorkshire side were physically stronger and it was not the prettiest of games, a goal by right-back Bobby Wilson in 1-1 draw left Dundee in with a shout for the Elland Road return on May 14th. This time Scott was on from the start in the hope of exploiting his pace on the break but although the result remained in doubt due to a fine performance from the Dark Blues, a late goal by Eddie Gray took Leeds into the final which they went on to win against Hungarian club Ferencvaros.

However, if the '67/8 season - with an American tour in the summer, the excitement of European football and a thrilling run to the Scottish League Cup Final - had been memorable, then the next two years would go a long way towards laying firm foundations in both the footballing career and the personal life of Jocky Scott.

Dundee got off to another good start in season 1968-69, qualifying from their League Cup section which included Hearts, Kilmarnock and Airdrie before a blitzkrieg performance swept away Division Two club Stranraer with an overwhelming 10-0 aggregate victory in the quarter-finals. Scott, who had netted his first-ever hat-trick for the club, commented: "That left us just 90 minutes away from a second successive League Cup Final appearance with Hibernian the only barrier to us making a Hampden return."

"The semi-final was played at Tynecastle on Wednesday, October 9th and with both clubs getting great backing from their fans in the 19,700 crowd, it turned out a real thriller," said Scott. "George McLean gave us an early lead only for Colin Stein to equalise almost immediately. But with Alan McGraw hirpling on the wing with a knee injury as Hibs had already used their substitute, it looked just a matter of time before we finished them off. So, it was a real blow when McGraw slid through the mud to poke the ball in right at the death. We were devastated."

That had been a shock but in another surprise move, Bobby Ancell resigned, with former Arbroath, Clyde and Falkirk boss John Prentice, who had briefly managed Scotland in 1966, taking over as Dundee manager. Prentice (42), who been recommended by Ancell, had done a particularly impressive job at Clyde. But although the outgoing boss, who at 56 years of age felt it was a job for a younger man, had hoped to continue in a lesser role as a youth coach, he soon found himself squeezed out of the picture.

Ancell had rebuilt the team since 1965 and in addition to the three good cup runs of the past year, had again shown his willingness to give youth a chance. Players like Ally Donaldson, Bobby Wilson, Steve Murray, Doug Houston, George Stewart, Alex Kinninmonth were amongst those who had been successfully groomed and now, for the first time in his professional career, Jocky Scott also could term himself a first-team regular.

Scott had made a devastating start to the season, combining brilliantly with Dens debutant John Duncan - a tall centre-forward and product of the local Butterburn YC - and scoring twice as he tore the Kilmarnock defence to pieces with his fast, darting runs. Of course, the stocky, dark-haired striker would not always have as much space in which to operate and he faced increased competition for a place from ex-Clyde striker Joe Gilroy, who had been signed from Fulham for £15,000, as well as the mercurial George McLean.

However, by the end of the '68/9 campaign Scott had made over 40 appearances and just as significantly finished Dundee's top scorer with 17 goals. "Of course I was pleased to finish top scorer but in January George McLean was transferred to Dunfermline after we got knocked out of the Scottish Cup by Hearts. So who knows what would have happened had he stayed. We'd slipped back to ninth in the league which was unacceptable to club and fans alike but we had a good nucleus of players and John Prentice wanted to build on this while adapting us to his own ideas, which included 4-3-3 and 4-4-2 formations."

"Doug Houston was an influential player at Dens and helped Prentice get his views across. He played a lot of games at outside-left in the European Cup season of '62/3 after arriving from Queen's Park as a part-timer before qualifying as a PE teacher from Jordanhill College. Perhaps because of that, it took him longer to establish himself but he could play equally well at left-back, in central defence or in midfield. He was great team player and a really good example to younger players."

"Steve Murray was another key man for the club at this time. He'd made his name at Dundee's public trial in 1963 and was a real perpetual motion midfielder, the push and run type with loads of stamina. He rarely wasted a pass and took over as captain after Alex Stuart began to struggle with injuries. Unfortunately, the club had to sell him to Aberdeen in 1970 to balance the books and he did well there before Jock Stein signed him for Celtic a few years later."

Away from football, Jocky Scott was by then well settled in the Dundee area. And, having met Elaine at the Chalet Roadhouse dance hall in Broughty Ferry two years earlier, the couple, with team-mate Ron Selway as Scott's best man, were married at St Lukes Church, Lochee on June 21st, 1969. As with every successful man there is a woman, and Scott acknowledges the part Elaine has played in his success: "The life of a footballer's wife, or worse still a football manager's wife, can be a lonely one, but fortunately Elaine has always understood and supported me in my career and still does."

The next best thing to happen to Scott - this time in his football career - occurred just three months later. For, with Dundee making an indifferent start to the 1969-70 season, and in dire need of additional punch up front after Joe Gilroy failed to make much impact, John Prentice paid £14,500 to bring Raith Rovers centre-forward Gordon Wallace to Dens. Wallace was a Dundonian who had been a Dens Park provisional signing nine years earlier but had never been called up. Instead, he had dropped down to Division Two to play for Montrose before moving on to Kirkcaldy where his continued scoring exploits - 30 goals for Raith who were struggling in Division One - saw him earn Scotland's prestigious Player of the Year award in 1968.

That was the first time a player from outwith the Old Firm had won the honour but, good as Wallace was at finding the net, he was far more than that. The centre was a master at holding the ball up and linking play and Scott would benefit greatly from his well-timed, accurate lay-offs and unselfish decoy runs with the pair destined to become one of the deadliest striking partnerships in Scotland.

"It was one of those things. We got on well almost from day one and we both had similar ideas in creating space and movement. Gordon was such an intelligent player with a fantastic positional sense and it suited me better to come from slightly deeper as I couldn't be picked up as easily. He had an amazing goal-scoring record in post-war Scottish football, bettered, I believe, by only a handful of other players such as Ally McCoist of Rangers and Henrik Larsson of Celtic."

"He was the missing link we had lacked. His arrival allowed Prentice to hold back John Duncan and bring him on in the reserves. Gordon finished top scorer with 23 goals, twice as many as me that year, and as well as help-ing us to sixth place, he helped us get past Airdrie and East Fife to reach the Scottish Cup semi-final in March 1970. Aberdeen met Kilmarnock in the other tie while we had the bad luck to get Celtic, who were heading for their second European Cup Final in three years, this time against Feyenoord, after a run that took them past Basle, Benfica, Fiorentina and Leeds United. That is what we were up against," sighed Scott.

"They were a really good team with bags of pace but despite going behind, Gordon Wallace put us level with a well taken shot. What we needed was a bit of luck but we rarely seemed to get it against them and with Ally Donaldson unfortunate not to hold a shot near the end, Lennox was right there to score. You couldn't help but feel sorry for big Ally. He was one of the mainstays of that team and was actually the back-up goalkeeper for Pat Liney in the championship-winning season of '61/62."

"Ally had a great physique for a goalie, big but fast on his feet and dominant and he picked up a number of Scottish League and Under-23 International caps. John Arrol challenged him strongly for the jersey for a couple of years but Ally eventually made the position his own. If I've got to be critical, sometimes his failure to let defenders know he was coming out let him down as we lost quite a few own-goals through Jim Easton and George Stewart pass-backs!"

Chapter 5

Poetry in Motion

The summer of 1970 was significant for a number of reasons. At the World Cup Finals in Mexico, the brilliant attacking play of the Brazilian quintet of Jairzinho, Pele, Tostao, Gerson and Rivelino had transfixed football fans all across the globe. But although the appointment of new Dens coach Jim McLean was of far less significance, his impact on Dundee Football Club and Jocky Scott was to be considerable. In those days, clubs had a trainer or coach rather than the modern-day assistant-manager, though the concept was much the same with the incumbent acting as the manager's right-hand man.

Bobby Seith had built up a fine reputation as Dundee coach before joining Rangers and later going on to manage Preston North End and Hearts. In 1966, Bruce Hay took his place at Dens and two years later he was reunited with John Prentice, who had been manager of Clyde for much of his time there. Hay, though, had now gone to South Africa and the vacancy was filled by ex-Clyde and Dundee player Jim McLean, who had hung up his boots after two years at Kilmarnock to become a tracksuit coach at Dens.

"In his three years at Dens, Jim McLean had been a fine footballer and was top scorer in '66/7 but he was never fully appreciated by many of fans. At one point, he endured barracking from a section of the support - as had I to a lesser extent - and reacted badly to it. No-one had really anticipated him going on to become a coach but we were glad to see him back. There was to be no old pals act but although he wasn't slow to crack the whip, he soon gained our respect and would have a very positive influence," said Scott.

As the season unfolded, it soon became clear that there was a new energy about the team. And although Dundee failed to progress beyond the quarter-final stage of the two domestic cup competitions, a fifth-place finish and a UEFA Cup place were testimony to the ongoing progress at Dens Park. Just as importantly, the conveyor-belt of young talent had continued in the shape of Jim Steele, Dave Johnston and Iain Phillip, with John Duncan, too, starting to fulfil his early promise.

Jocky Scott recalled their emergence on the first-team scene: "Jim Steele was a rangy, red-headed midfielder with attitude, while Dave "Biffo" Johnston, was a tough-tackling left-back groomed to replace Bobby Cox who had retired in 1969. Both started off by wearing the number 11 jersey, albeit in a withdrawn left-wing role to give them a taste of first-team football. "Steely" quickly established himself as a no-holds barred midfielder and he soon became a bit of a cult hero with the fans."

"Iain Phillip was a very different style of player, a tall, elegant and effective central defender, a really classy player who exuded style and composure. At times, John Prentice would play with three at the back and, dependant on the opposition, use any three of Phillip, Stewart, Houston or Steele with the other deployed elsewhere. Then our full-backs Bobby Wilson and Davie Johnston had the freedom to come forward and give us penetration down the flanks," said Scott. "It worked a treat and in many ways, Prentice was ahead of his time tactically."

All this, of course, would have been to no avail without a cutting edge up front but Dundee had Wallace and Scott, a partnership that was to flourish even more under the watchful eye of Jim McLean. Indeed, there was now a near telepathic understanding between the pair, as appreciated by Gordon Gray in *The Peoples Journal* after a 4-1 romp over Ayr United: "The Gordon Wallace - Jocky Scott partnership which promised so much in the past struck gold on Wednesday night." Dick Donnelly of *The Scottish Sunday Express* was another admirer and following a crushing 5-1 win over Cowdenbeath at Dens, he declared: "Cowden had no answer to Dundee's twin spearhead of Gordon Wallace and Jocky Scott!"

Jocky Scott ended the '70/1 campaign as top scorer on 21 goals, Wallace on seven less, with young John Duncan contributing 15 goals. Over the past two years, Scott had progressed immeasurably. Gone was the head-down, individualist of old and although the solo touches of brilliance still remained, the pacy Aberdonian had developed into a highly effective team player.

"Great Scott!" proclaimed *The Sunday Post* after a 2-0 League Cup victory over Kilmarnock, with the article continuing: "Dundee's talented number 10, Jocky Scott, was the man of the match with both goals. He is one of the most exciting players in the country. Time and again his speed off the mark threw Killie's rearguard into chaos and two goals were no more than he deserved!"

That was no isolated headline with Donnelly again lauding the Dens Park star after an end of season 4-0 drubbing of Motherwell at Dens as he enthused: *"Scott - the Dundee man with Sparkle!"* Scott's scoring exploits had been duly noted and in summer 1971, the fleet-footed Dens Park star was invited to join the Scotland squad for the two-game tour of Denmark and the USSR. The national team boss was Bobby Brown, formerly manager of St Johnstone. He had been in charge since 1967 but was coming under increasing pressure as Scotland had lost four out of their last five internationals.

A number of players had withdrawn from the tour but Scott was only too delighted to be involved: "On June 9th, I substituted for Aberdeen forward Jim Forrest for the last quarter of an hour at the Idraetsparken in Copenhagen. However, Denmark, who included Erik Sorensen, Preben Arentoft, and Mogens Berg, who I'd played against when they were at Morton and Dundee United, held on to win 1-0. Five days later, I got my second full cap when I started wide on the left against the USSR in Dynamo Moscow's Lenin Stadium but with only 20,000 in the 100,000-capacity stadium, almost half as many as there had been in Copenhagen, there wasn't much of an atmosphere."

Scotland - Clark (Aberdeen); Brownlie (Hibs), Munro (Wolves), McKinnon (Rangers), Dickson (Kilmarnock); Forrest (Aberdeen), Watson (Motherwell), Stanton (Hibs), Scott (Dundee); Stein (Rangers), Robb (Aberdeen), with Hugh Curran of Wolves later replacing Stein. However, once again, they went down to the only goal of the game, scored after 25 minutes, although newspapers credited Scott as having a fine game.

Unfortunately for him, that was to be Bobby Brown's last game in charge of Scotland. The new boss was none other than Tommy Docherty who had released him as a youngster at Chelsea and, effectively, Jocky Scott's international career was over. The Dens star was philosophic: "Playing for Scotland was my proudest moment and I thought I'd done well enough to merit another chance. Circumstances dictated otherwise but I consoled myself in the realisation that there were plenty of other players, perhaps even better than myself, who were never capped."

But with the 1971-72 season fast approaching, Jocky Scott had little time for regrets. Prior to the Scotland tour, he had been in the Dens squad which participated in a Lisbon invitation tournament involving Sporting Lisbon, Atletico Madrid and Norwich City and, possibly with their latest European foray in mind, the club had also undertaken a four game pre-season trip to Belgium. Having reached the European Cup semi-final in 1963 and the same stage of the Fairs Cup in 1968, the Dark Blues had a proud European pedigree as Scott recalled: "It was great to get back into Europe after a three-year absence."

"We first defeated AB Copenhagen 4-2 at Dens and John Duncan finished them off with the only goal over there. We felt really comfortable playing against the continentals as our style of football just seemed ideal for it. And when the draw paired us with old European Cup foes Cologne, there was great excitement as tales of the famous 8-1 win against the second favourites and how Dundee survived a rough-house of a return to reach the next round 8-5 on aggregate were retold."

This time, the first leg took place in West Germany, where Dundee were well treated and Alex Kinninmonth grabbed a valuable consolation goal in a 2-1 defeat. That left the tie finely poised and the second leg proved a footballing classic: "John Duncan headed us in front but Cologne, who were a very good side, hit back twice to lead 4-2 on aggregate with half-an-hour left," said Scott. "That was a real shaker and things went flat as we then needed three goals to go through, but when we got a second on 69 minutes the Dens Park crowd got right behind us."

"I've never experienced an atmosphere quite like that though Andy Penman had told me what it was like when Dundee recovered to beat Raith Rovers 5-4 at Dens in the title-winning season. We knew we could do it, the crowd knew we were up for it and it was just attack after attack, although Cologne remained lethal on the break. Just six minutes remained when John Duncan fired in the equaliser for his hat-trick and the whole place went nuts! We were shooting into the TC Keay end, where we had them penned in."

"It was like the Alamo and with time rapidly running out we got another corner. There must have been about 19 players in their penalty box and it turned into the biggest goalmouth scramble of all time. First Jim Steele, then John Duncan had shots blocked on the line before Bobby Wilson reacted first to crash in the winner from just a few yards out!"

"It was a sensational comeback and probably the most exciting game I ever played in. After the final whistle, the players hugged each other and rolled on the ground delirious with joy as Dundee fans invaded the field. A couple of Cologne players - one was the West German international Wolfgang Overath - were led from the field in tears, saying they couldn't believe they had lost. Still on a high, I replied that it was because we'd scored more goals. Hardly a consolation for him but it really was a full-on adrenalin rush at full-time!"

Having recently faced former European Cup adversaries Sporting Lisbon and Cologne, it was entirely fitting that the Dark Blues were then paired with Italian giants AC Milan as Scott acknowledged: "Once again we were treading in the footsteps of the past. It was just incredible walking out into the great bowl of the San Siro in the first leg in Italy. We had Iain Phillip operating as a sweeper behind a back four and were doing fine until big George Stewart scored yet another own goal and we went on to lose 3-0."

Back at Dens, Gordon Wallace reduced the deficit with a header before half-time but although John Duncan added a second, the dynamic Dark Blues could not find a way through the embattled Milan defence. "Dundee played superbly well and Prentice again showed his tactical nous by switching young Duncan Lambie, usually a fast, old-fashioned left-winger, inside, and from there he tore the Italians apart. There was another great atmosphere and all we lacked that night was a bit of luck, said Scott."

There would be no tangible success for Scott's team that season, though there were a number of other memorable matches. In September, the Dark Blues finally ended a six-game spell without a win against city rivals Dundee United by beating them 6-4 for their first Dens derby success since 1962. "We often played well against United but couldn't get a result though we felt we had the better squad and were always confident of winning. It just never seemed to happen for us," explained Scott. However, that trend had been broken in spectacular style with Dundee turning on an exhilarating brand of football in a 10-goal derby spectacular.

"Two goals apiece from Gordon Wallace, Alex Bryce and myself gave us a 6-2 lead with 10 minutes left but we eased off and they got two late goals. Alex Bryce was a brilliant ball-player on his day and he gave them a torrid time," said Scott. But this was no one-man show for Dundee had threatened a slaughter as their fast, man to man play tore the visitors apart.

Inevitably, buzz-bomb Scott had played his part, netting a coolly struck penalty and later, after evading three desperate challenges, he tormented the United defenders by dwelling on the ball just long enough for them to rush back before netting from point-blank range. It was a moment to savour for Scott and Dundee supporters alike!

For anyone who had not seen the rivals since April 1969, there would have been a surprise. Since returning from a second trip to the USA to represent Dallas Tornado, United had shelved their long-standing colours of black and white. Instead they had adopted tangerine and black, while since 1971 Dundee had sported a crisp all-white jersey with dark blue shorts and red socks as their first-team colours and it would be another two years before they reverted to the traditional dark blue jerseys.

On the pitch, it had been a particularly good year for Scott and there was also the thrill of another close-season tour, this time to far-off New Zealand and Australia. There, he and pool - of the green baize variety - partner Gordon Wallace were rebranded "The Hustlers" after the recent film of that name starring Paul Newman who repeatedly cleaned up the table. For his part, Scott admitted: "We've won a few bucks but I don't think we'll ever earn a living with a cue!"

However, there had also been a couple of major upsets. In December 1971 had come news that the promising Dens Park managerial set-up was no more. John Prentice resigned with the intention of taking a post outwith the game, while Jim McLean, on learning that he was not to be Prentice's replacement, accepted the position of manager at nearby Dundee United.

Within a month, the inspirational Jim Steele was sold to Southampton for £72,000 and just eight months later Iain Phillip would follow him south to Crystal Palace for £95,000. All agreed that great progress has been made under Prentice and McLean and that the foundations for success were there, so their departure along with two of Dundee's top players had come as a massive blow.

"The pair of them made the whole club far more professional and the players responded on the field," said Scott. So, we were hugely disappointed when John Prentice left Dens Park and most of us wanted Jim McLean to succeed him."

"Many fans said that that Dundee side was the best since the halcyon days of the early '60s. Prentice was a tactician though to be honest some of his stuff just went over my head, whereas Jim McLean, who was closer to the players, could get his ideas over more easily," said Scott. "They were great together though and to be honest, no disrespect to the new management team that came in, it was a huge blow to the players when McLean didn't get the job and moved across the road. Wee Jim made us fitter, worked on our touch, control and passing, but above all demanded a very high standard and woe betide anyone who didn't consistently perform to his potential."

"What he achieved over there - two League Cup wins, a League Champ-ionship, various cup final appearances and regular participation in European competition - was remarkable and altered the balance of football power in the city. But Jim admitted that he had left a much more talented squad at Dens than he inherited at United. And I have no doubt that things would have been very different for us had he stayed, said Scott."

McLean indeed proved himself one of the great Scottish managers prompting Dundee supporters to question why he had been allowed to leave Dens Park. Many years later ex-Dundee FC chairman Ian Gellatly would ruefully admit that he had accepted the advice of outgoing manager John Prentice that McLean the coach was not ready to make the step up to manager. It also emerged that there had been a rift between Gellatly and McLean dating from the aftermath of the 1967 League Cup Final when words were exchanged, though this had not prevented McLean's return as coach in 1970.

There is, however, another instance where John Prentice's judgement might be called into question. In 1973 he returned from Canada to manage Falkirk, where one of his players was none other than Alex Ferguson, the former St Johnstone, Dunfermline and Rangers centre-forward. By then Ferguson was player-coach in charge of first-team training sessions but Prentice was quick to relieve him of his coaching duties, though it is unclear whether he felt his own authority was being undermined or if he believed Ferguson unsuitable for coaching.

Soon afterwards, Ferguson was transferred to Ayr United; within a year he had taken charge of East Stirling and his path to managerial greatness had begun. Perhaps, therefore, it could be said that Prentice's judgment was twice flawed, or just that he felt a further learning curve was required to convert what he may have seen as "raw material" into the finished article of a football manager. But either way, Dundee's loss was Dundee United's gain.

Chapter 6

Days in the Sun

In January 1972, Davie White became the new Dundee manager with Harold Davis as his assistant. A Clyde player for eight years, White had become player-coach at Shawfield in 1965 before replacing John Prentice who was made Scotland boss in March 1966. White did well, taking the "Bully Wee" from eleventh place in '65/6 to third in '66/7, progress which saw him named assistant-manager to Scott Symon at Rangers.

However, just five months later the long-serving Symon was axed and White took over as manager. It proved too swift an elevation for despite his tactical abilities, White, who was still in his mid-30s, had no international experience and encountered disciplinary problems with big-name players like Jim Baxter and Willie Henderson. Just as significantly, he was unable to topple Celtic from the pinnacle of Scottish football and in late 1969 he was sacked.

Interestingly, Davie White and Jim McLean had both been at Shawfield during John Prentice's spell as Clyde boss from March 1963 until McLean joined Dundee in September 1965. In 1966, another ex-Clyde star, midfielder Alex Bryce, came to Dens and Prentice's appointment, then the arrival of coach Maurice Friel, Joe Gilroy and defensive veterans Jim "Bonzo" Fraser and Davie Souter - the last two had also been with Prentice at Arbroath - had further swelled the contingent of former Clyde personnel.

Davie White had a good knowledge of the Scottish game as well as his own tactical ideas and although Harold Davis was an old-fashioned trainer, White was always on hand to provide his coaching input. Senior players like Doug Houston and Gordon Wallace, too, had their views and on occasion, there were lively discussions. On analysing Dundee's chances for the new season, the new boss had remarked: "I'm expecting a lot from Jocky Scott. He's now an experienced player of 24, an internationalist and on his day a world-beater. But I want more application from him, more concentration. He'll have to curb his tendency to go out of the game for long spells."

Any disappointment the players may have felt at the departure of the previous management team was not reflected in their on-field performances, Dundee ending the '71/2 campaign fifth and losing just two of their opening 12 games in 1972-73. Jocky Scott had responded well to White's challenge and he recalled: "That run included a 2-0 victory over Celtic at Dens in September, the first time we'd beaten them in seven years. Yet within days Iain Phillip was off to Crystal Palace. The fans were angry and I read one letter in *The Scottish Sunday Mail* where the writer said he would not be surprised if Dundee began to line up with price tags on their backs! For my part, I was pleased for Iain but annoyed at seeing a good team dismantled. I was also upset that my own loyalty had never been rewarded and asked for a transfer."

In *The Scottish Daily Express*, John McKenzie - *"The Voice of Football"* - was quick to profer his opinion: "Jocky Scott is one of football's characters. When he is switched on as he was against Celtic, he can be a highly profit-able attacking midfielder. He can be useful as an attacker as well. I once saw him turn it on for Scotland as a left-winger in Russia, about the only player in dark blue who did so. He can be moody, he can hide in a game if it is not his day. But he is a character and the roar of anticipation and encouragement that rose from the crowd every time he got the ball at the recent Hibs game should sound alarm bells for the Dens Park board!"

Scott in fact hadn't particularly wanted to move and stated his willingness to play out the rest of his days with Dundee. Clearly, the solution was a new long-term contract on improved financial terms, and having recently achieved a degree of financial stability and in the knowledge that Rangers had expressed an interest, the Dundee directors pushed out the boat to satisfy Scott's wishes.

"I was delighted and it actually turned out a really good if ultimately frustrating season. The foundations for success were there with Bobby Ford and the more recently acquired Bobby Robinson - like Ford, a former Falkirk midfielder – and ex-Hibs keeper Thomson Allan, coming to the fore. "We'd scored 111 goals in domestic competition, our highest total in nine years, were unbeaten at Dens all season, and actually went 29 home games undefeated between May '72 and September '73," explained Scott.

"By that time, John Duncan - nicknamed "Gillie" after the famous Alan Gilzean due to his own considerable aerial prowess - had matured into a top-class striker. So we then had three excellent finishers, were able to alternate the striking roles with one playing a bit deeper or wider, and the goals really began to flow. Gordon Wallace and myself both got 18 but big John got a remarkable 40 goals - including five in a League Cup tie against East Stirling - and earned himself a Scottish League cap against England."

"We weren't consistent enough to challenge in the league but felt that with a little luck we could win a cup. In the League Cup quarter-final, we beat Celtic 1-0 at Dens then lost 3-2 at Parkhead, where I caught the ball perfectly to score a 25-yard thunderbolt – for some reason it was live on STV - only to lose the Hampden play-off 4-1 (after Scott himself had put them ahead). We'd high hopes of going all the way in the Scottish, knocking in goals galore to crush Dunfermline, Stranraer and Montrose en route to the semis. But Celtic - who we'd beaten twice that season - proved an insurmountable barrier. We held them to 0-0 before 53,000 at Hampden and after 90 minutes

34

of the replay there was again no scoring. We played really well in the second half but in the end they got three goals in extra-time and that was that!

Scott, though, was playing some of the best football of his career as described by Dick Donnelly in *The Scottish Sunday Express*: "Montrose's hopes of cup glory were dashed by a thoroughly professional Dundee performance highlighted by a superb individual display from international forward Jocky Scott. With a personal tally of two goals and a couple of assists, Scott was their main tormentor but I can think of few defences in the land who could have halted the rampant inside-forward as he repeatedly ripped the home defence apart with dynamic runs from midfield."

In football, though, nothing can be taken for granted and a few months earlier, Scott was very much the villain when his slack pass-back caught out keeper Thomson Allan at Gayfield. *"Misery for Jocky Scott,"* screamed the headlines as the story continued: "Poor Jocky. On his day, Scott is unquestionably one of the finest players around. But unfortunately in this one he suffered the triple ignominy of being hustled out of the game by John Fletcher, scoring the own-goal which gave Arbroath their win, and finally being substituted seven minutes from the end."

However, success for Jocky Scott and the Dark Blues was just around the corner: "It was clear we had bags of talent and despite losing skipper Doug Houston to Rangers, Davie White did well to bring in Tommy Gemmell on a free transfer from Nottingham Forest. Here was a guy who'd gained 18 full caps for Scotland and performed at the very highest level, playing and scoring in two European Cup Finals, one of only two British players to do so, as well as playing in the World Club Championship. He was a natural leader and also brought a certain confidence and hardness that we'd probably lacked."

"We topped our 1973 League Cup section finishing above St Johnstone, Hearts and Partick Thistle but then made heavy weather of getting past Dunfermline (5-4), and Clyde (3-2), in home and away ties to reach the last four. Too many goals were being conceded and on hearing he wanted back to Scotland, Davie White managed to re-sign Iain Phillip from Crystal Palace for half what Dundee had received. His return settled the defence and for once we got a favourable semi-final draw, against Kilmarnock - then a Division Two club - with the Old Firm contesting the other tie."

The semi-final tie was played on a Wednesday evening in late November. But Britain was in the midst of an energy crisis with severe power shortages at home and in the workplace reducing many to a three-day working week and there were only 4,682 fans within the vast expanse of the then 100,000-capacity Hampden Park. Surprisingly, the Scottish League had not opted for an afternoon kick-off and with the floodlights, powered by a motor generator rather than the national grid, producing just a third of their normal output, there was a ghostly atmosphere around the sparsely-populated stadium as inspirational skipper Tommy Gemmell fired home a hard low shot for the only goal of the game.

"So there we were in the final - against Celtic - for the first time since 1967, yet unlike so many other great performances in recent years, we'd hardly kicked a ball! And rather than the traditional date of late October, the League Cup Final would go ahead on Saturday December 15th, right in the depths of winter! Nevertheless, we looked forward to it, though blizzard conditions in the days leading up to the final meant training was restricted and put the occasion itself in doubt."

Previewing the final, Tommy Gallacher, who was chief football writer for *The Courier* and a member of Dundee's League Cup winning side of 1951, concluded: "Dundee have everything to gain and nothing to lose as Celtic are strong favourites, though they have lost the last three League Cup Finals against Hibs, Partick Thistle and Rangers. Skill-wise, there is really little between them though Dundee sometimes tend to look on Celtic as some kind of supermen and when things go wrong, accept the inevitable. However, they now have Tommy Gemmell and he knows what winning is all about."

"That morning, there were grave doubts whether the game would be played," recalled Jocky Scott. It took three hours for our coach to reach Glasgow through snowbound roads. There was no Perth to Stirling motorway back then, so to avoid towns we went via Kinross and Kincardine, stopping at the Dutch Inn at Skinflats. The restaurant, which was owned by well-known former Falkirk full-back Jimmy McIntosh, was one of the best Steakhouses in Scotland but with no time to linger, we managed just a 25 minute stop for a hurried pre-match meal. It was hardly ideal preparation for a cup final but on reflection it may have worked in our favour as there was little time to get nervous and in any case, most of us thought the match would be off."

"When we got to Hampden, snow and slush lay on the pitch and neither club wanted the game played. But, after a late inspection, referee Bobby Davidson - never a favourite figure with Celtic boss Jock Stein - deemed that the game should go ahead. And having checked the pitch with the rest of the Dundee players, I opted for longer studs rather than rubbers to try and get some grip on what was clearly a hazardous surface."

To limit the use of floodlights and conserve power, Saturday afternoon kick-offs had been brought forward by an hour but to allow for extra-time, the final began at 1.30pm. Dundee had brought 16 players but with the exception of Gordon Wallace, who passed a late fitness test along with George Stewart, they fielded their successful semi-final side. Mike Hewitt, Alec Pringle and Jimmy Wilson were the unlucky trio who took their place in the stand, disappointingly for Wilson who had played against Killie. But with a question remaining over Wallace's fitness, another striker, Ian Scott, was preferred for a place on the bench.

The teams lined up: *Dundee - Allan; Wilson R, Stewart, Phillip, Gemmell; Robinson, Ford, Lambie; Duncan, Wallace, Scott J. Subs. - Johnston, Scott I. Celtic - Hunter; McGrain, McNeill, McCluskey, Brogan; Murray, Hay, Callaghan; Wilson, Hood, Dalglish. Subs. - Johnstone, Connelly.*

A Scottish League Cup Final record low attendance of 27,974 fans braved the snow and sleet to watch the game with thousands huddled around the unprotected Hampden terracings with miserable conditions underfoot. Initially, the pitch was bone hard but as the sleet turned to driving rain, the surface turned to slush before becoming saturated with water. Nevertheless, it was to prove a memorable afternoon for the Dark Blues with fitness doubt Gordon Wallace the hero of the day!

Later, in *The Scottish Sunday Express*, Harry Andrew described the action: "In the first half, Duncan shot over with a great chance, Hunter made a superb save from Wallace and again from Scott. Wilson shot wide for Celtic, then Ford blasted over with the goal gaping. After the interval, Dalglish brought out the save of the match from Allan and Wilson again shot past the post. But from then, the sides found it harder and harder to create chances as conditions deteriorated - until 14 minutes from the end."

"Just over the halfway line, Bobby Wilson launched a free-kick into the Celtic penalty box. Straight it flew to Gordon Wallace facing his own goal. He gathered, all in one smooth movement, and cracked the ball low into the back of the net! And that was it despite a couple of anxious moments towards the end. It was a climax that no work of fiction could have bettered. The fairy-tale truth is that Gordon fought all week against an ankle injury to get fit for his big moment. But he made it at the last gasp and how he and all Dundee must rejoice over that fact today!"

Appropriately, the *Express* headlines read: *"Centre Beats Injury To End Dundee's 21-Year Wait,"* while, in his Monday column, Hugh Taylor of *The Daily Record* also applauded Wallace's winner: "It was a spectacular goal that Pele would have envied and brought desperately needed glamour as well as victory for Dundee in the League Cup Final at Hampden. Neither is there any argument that Dundee deserved to win the League Cup. They were the better, sharper, and more flexible team, deadly on the break and making fine use of the ball."

The Sporting Post also hailed Dundee's success and was full of praise for Tommy Gemmell's role in the success: "Dundee's cavalier captain was a constant inspiration. He laughed and splashed his way through an inspiring performance even when derision was howled at him from some Celtic fans." Tommy Gallacher, too, was full of praise for the Dark Blues in *The Courier*: "Some of the stuff they produced, especially in the first-half was of similar vintage to the champagne they were to drink later at a celebration dinner laid on by the club. It was superb and it was apparent then as Dundee stroked the ball around from man to man that this would pay bigger dividends than Celtic's method of running with the ball in conditions which were all against it."

It was an occasion that would forever be etched in Scott's memory: "That was the first time I had won anything and I savoured the moment. Celtic probably had more of the game without dominating but we were really dangerous on the break and I always felt we could nick one. It was a bit hectic towards the end but we defended well and our luck held. In the last minute, wee Jimmy Johnstone went down in the box but the ref waved it away and later it was seen that he'd tripped over Kenny Dalglish's leg! Going up the Hampden steps to collect a winner's medal was amazing. What a fantastic feeling!

"In goal, Thomson Allan was immaculate despite the difficult conditions, while big Tam led by example at the back. He and Bobby Wilson got forward when they could while Ian Phillip remained resolute alongside George Stewart who had to get four stitches in his mouth following an early collision. In midfield, Bobby Ford, Bobby Robinson and Duncan Lambie were constantly on the move, shutting down moves and attacking when possible. Ford was a battler - though that belied his skill - and perfectly complemented the more creative Robinson and the direct running of Lambie. Conditions were far from ideal for forwards but myself, John Duncan and Gordon Wallace kept interchanging to keep the Celtic defenders on their toes – and of course keep ourselves warm!"

"The game ended around 3.15pm and by the time we got presented with the Cup and took it to the fans – we took perhaps only 3,000 or 4,000 that day due to the weather, it must have been around 4.30pm before we got out of Hampden. So it was perhaps 7 o'clock before the coach got back to Dundee, where we got a great welcome from the fans in the snow-covered streets, though there was no victory parade as it had been far from certain that the game would go ahead."

So what was that League Cup win worth to the Dundee players? "I'm often asked that question and when I say that we got £500 a man, people are somewhat surprised. However, £500 was decent money back in 1973 when average earnings in the UK was just over £1,900 per annum," said Scott.

"That evening, players and officials attended a celebration dinner at the Angus Hotel on the corner of the Overgate in Dundee. It was a wonderful, carefree occasion and needless to say, a lot of celebrating was done! Later on - I think it was big George Stewart's suggestion - we thought it might be a nice touch to pay our ex-coach Jim McLean a visit as he had done so much for us during his time at Dens. About six or seven of us went to his house in Broughty Ferry but word got back to Davie White who was none too pleased.

It wasn't meant to be a snub to him but I suppose paying a visit to someone who was the manager of your city rivals was a daft thing to do and we were all fined."

Winning the League Cup had been a major breakthrough and despite the less than glamorous circumstances, the Dens Parkers had greatly gained in self-belief. "Soon afterwards, we were back in cup action – this time in the Scottish Cup – and this really was a fantastic spell for Dundee. In the first round, we were away to Aberdeen and although they had slipped back from a few years earlier, they remained formidable at Pittodrie where we had struggled in recent years," said Scott.

"However, we competed well, got a break when Davie Johnston's long-range shot was deflected past Bobby Clark and Bobby Robinson finished them off with a second. It was a big moment for Davie, an Aberdonian like myself, and with wee Jimmy Wilson having previously played for the Dons, the three of us had extra cause for celebration! Because of the continuing energy crisis, the football authorities had experimented with Sunday football so that tie took place on a Sunday before almost 24,000. Bumper attendances turned out all across the country and this was the start of our famous "Month of Sundays" when we won four successive games culminating in a 3-0 win over Rangers before a massive 65,000 crowd at Ibrox!"

"Going to Glasgow was always daunting but although we were the under-dogs, we fancied our chances, particularly as we'd beaten Celtic 2-1 at Parkhead the week before," Scott went on. In the first half, Rangers put Dundee under real pressure but five minutes after the restart, Jimmy Wilson got to the bye-line and from his cut-back, Jocky Scott rifled the ball home. It had been a goal of real quality and with confidence beginning to ooze throughout the team, a further two goals by John Duncan ensured a comprehensive victory and a place in the last eight.

Scott had invariably excelled in games against the Light Blues and for a good spell Dundee had been a real thorn in their side: "I loved the big games like the derbies against United and against both of the Old Firm. We did really well against Rangers, beating them at Dens four years out of five between 1968 and 1972 with the odd win at Ibrox and as I recall, I got my share of the goals against them!"

"In the quarter final, we got another tough one - at Easter Road against Eddie Turnbull's enterprising Hibs side who were having a great season. Well, we had won the League Cup and were bang in form too, so this really was one for the football purists. I put us ahead and it then became an absolute thriller of a game which ebbed and flowed before ending 3-3. It was breath-taking stuff - they had the likes of Stanton, Blackley, Cropley, Gordon and Harper while we weren't too bad ourselves! That night the game was shown on TV and many people later asked what became of the archive footage which later disappeared as did most of the '73 League Cup Final and other big games such as the UEFA Cup tie against Cologne".

"Around 28,000 were there, but such was the cup-tie fever that almost 31,000 turned out for the Dens Park replay, the most I'd played in front of at Dens since the 33,000 at the Scottish Cup tie against Rangers in 1968. We gave our fans plenty to cheer about that evening and I got one, Johnny Duncan and Bobby Wilson the others in a 3-0 triumph as we took them apart with a devastating first-half performance. We, as well as many others, thought our name was on the Scottish Cup that year," said Scott. "Celtic, Hearts and Dundee United were the other teams left, but as luck would have it we again - as in 1970 and 1973 - got Celtic, who remained the top team in Scotland."

Not much got past Jock Stein and, noting the influence of Scott, the uncompromising Jim Brogan was handed a man-marking job. It would be fair to say that Celtic were determined not to allow Dundee to play their normal expansive game and before a crowd of 58,000, referee Grant appeared unwilling to curtail their very physical approach. John Duncan took a constant buffeting from Billy McNeill but it was the Dundee man who ended up in the book after only his first foul. Scott, too, got the treatment and with the Dark Blues unable to get into their usual flow, their double dream died when Jimmy Johnstone netted a 44th minute goal to put the Parkhead club through to the final.

It was a sad recollection for Scott: "I always found Jim Brogan a difficult opponent. At the time, there was no better man-marker in the Scottish game and that night he certainly let me know he was around! Having lost just two of our previous 15 games, we certainly believed we could make it a cup double. I'm sure we would have beaten either Hearts or United but nothing came off for us that evening against Celtic, who had the huge advantage of having the semi-final played in Glasgow in midweek and unfortunately our opportunity had gone."

Nevertheless, it had been a memorable season for Dundee and Scott in particular, who went on to amass his highest-ever total of 29 goals. Highlights had included a four-goal haul in the 5-2 mauling of Arbroath - who included Scott's mentor and former Dens Park great, Andy Penman - a hat-trick against East Fife and a double in a 2-1 league win over Rangers at Ibrox, the latter giving Dundee a dandy double against the Old Firm in Glasgow that term, as well as their decisive Scottish Cup victory over the Light Blues.

The brilliant play of Scott had not gone unnoticed by Scotland boss Willie Ormond, who had succeeded Tommy Docherty in 1973. But although Scott and strike partner John Duncan were named along with Bobby Robinson and Thomson Allan in a 40-man preliminary squad, only the Dundee goalkeeper was included in the final squad of 22 who made the trip to the World Cup Finals in West Germany in June 1974.

Up front, the Scots would select from veteran striker Denis Law, Peter Lorimer, Kenny Dalglish, Joe Jordan or Donald Ford, while as attacking midfielders, they had Jimmy Johnstone, Willie Morgan, Tommy Hutchison and Peter Cormack. However, although Scotland performed well and were unbeaten, they returned home having failed to qualify from the group stages.

Next season, 1974-75, Dundee would again finish in the top five and once more reach the semi-finals of the Scottish Cup. As Scott recalled: "For the third consecutive season it was Celtic - rather than Airdrie or Motherwell! I suppose some might think we had a mental block when playing them but they remained a really good side and were especially difficult to beat at Hampden. We played some great football that night but still lost 1-0."

In Europe too, Dundee had hit the proverbial brick wall and unlike previous campaigns, they found themselves well off the pace, going out of the UEFA Cup at the first time of asking in both '73/74 and '74/75. Jocky Scott had been greatly impressed by Dutch side Twente Enschede in 1973: "We lost 3-1 at home, the first time Dundee had lost a European tie at Dens and I have to say we got a football lesson. We were a good side but this was total football like I had never seen before. Every player was comfortable on the ball and defenders could control and pass the ball as well as any of the forwards. In Holland we did well to keep the score to 4-2 and lost 7-3 on aggregate."

"I shouldn't have been that surprised, though, for Celtic had found the Dutchmen of Feyenoord too hot to handle back in 1970. And at the 1974 World Cup Finals, the proof was there for all to see as Holland gained millions of new admirers with their magnificent play en route to the final where they narrowly lost to West Germany. There were outstanding individuals like Johan Cruyff, Johan Neeskens and Wim van Hanegem but they fitted seamlessly into the team pattern and it was the flexibility, athleticism and movement of the players that was so impressive."

This then was modern football and when Dundee faced RWD (Racing White Deventer) of Molenbeek in October 1974, it was to be more of the same. The pacy Belgians, who operated very much in the Dutch style, left Dens Park with a 4-2 win for a 5-2 aggregate success and it would be another 29 years before Dundee made their next foray into Europe.

The '74/75 league campaign ended with a 2-0 home win over Hearts with Jocky Scott on the bench to allow the highly promising Gordon Strachan to make his full league debut. But although the popular Aberdonian came on to score, none of the fans could realise that it would be his last home league game in a dark blue jersey for quite some time.

41

Chapter 7

Tale of Two Cities

In **summer 1975**, there was a mood of optimism around Dens Park with the introduction of the new 10-team Premier League heralding a fresh dawn in Scottish football. For some time, the six biggest clubs in Scotland - Rangers, Celtic, Hearts, Hibs, Aberdeen and Dundee - had wanted change and by trimming the league from 18 teams, it was hoped to reduce the number of "meaningless games". Perhaps more to the point, home clubs would no longer share their gate money 50-50 but would retain all their receipts. However, with two clubs - 20% of the league - to be automatically relegated, few of them could have envisaged the troubles that lay ahead.

On paper, Dundee appeared to have a good squad but there was to be no repeat of their 1973 League Cup success as they ended third in a section containing Hibs, Ayr United and Dunfermline. The Easter Road side were rightly regarded as one of Scotland's top clubs, but Dundee's failure to finish above the two lesser lights ought to have had alarm bells ringing at Dens. Supporters were certainly not happy and in mid-August their mood darkened with the news that fans' favourite Jocky Scott - rated as worth £40,000 - had been transferred to Aberdeen in exchange for Dons winger Ian Purdie plus £15,000.

In his 11 seasons at Dens, Scott, who was not yet 28, had four times finished as the club's top scorer and in recent years had played the best football of his career. He had had his share of games on the July tours of Sweden and the Scottish Highlands but had been restricted to just one competitive appearance - against Motherwell in the Anglo-Scottish Cup - in Dundee's opening five games. The bustling striker had reportedly suffered a groin injury but his absence from the substitutes bench for the first three League Cup ties and the possibility of his becoming cup-tied, appeared to indicate he no longer featured in Davie White's plans, particularly as he went straight into the Aberdeen side on arriving at Pittodrie.

What then was the rationale behind the sale of one of the Dens Park club's three Scotland internationals - and to one of their nearest rivals? Certainly it was true that in the past six years, Dundee had lost to Celtic in Scottish Cup semi-finals four times but that compared favourably with most other provincial clubs as the Parkhead stranglehold on the Scottish game persisted. Following Dundee's most recent Hampden failure, manager White had pledged to rebuild the team while emphasising his belief in the promising youngsters at the club. However, little was he to realise the premium that would be put on experience in the new cut-throat Premier set-up.

The strongly-built striker Eric Sinclair and another 19-year-old, midfielder Gordon Strachan - the latter a precocious talent who had been voted Scottish Reserve Player of the Year for the past two seasons, were the most prominent of the youngsters. The ginger-haired midfielder had capped a great pre-season by performing brilliantly in a 2-1 friendly win over a star-studded Arsenal at Dens, where he had outshone the battle-hardened former England international Alan Ball.

One theory, then, was that White wanted to fast-track Strachan while Scott, perhaps unhappy at no longer being assured of a regular first-team jersey, had grabbed the opportunity of a move north. And when Dons boss Jimmy Bonthrone had made his move, White was happy to get decent value for Scott, with the left-sided Purdie bringing added pace to the Dens Park midfield.

Scott though had another theory: "I often wondered if Davie White determined to clear out all those involved in the Angus Hotel affair in December 1973. There was no doubt that we were wrong to leave the League Cup celebrations to visit Jim McLean. It was disrespectful to Davie and the rest of the squad and must have been hurtful for him too in view of what was believed to be a tenuous relationship with Jim McLean at Shawfield."

"Co-incidentally or not, most of these players - Duncan Lambie to St Johnstone (£15,000), John Duncan to Tottenham Hotspur (£140,000), both in October 1974, myself and Ian Scott (free transfer), in August 1975, and George Stewart, Gordon Wallace and Bobby Wilson, all in May 1976, were moved out of Dens Park in a relatively short time. Only Dave Johnston would remain - until his departure in 1978."

For Scott, then, there was some sadness at leaving Dens though it gave him the opportunity to play for his boyhood heroes. "I'd had the chance to sign for Aberdeen as a kid but turned it down as they were a club going nowhere," he said later. "There had, though, been good times under Eddie Turnbull and knowing their potential, I jumped at the chance to join my home town team the second time around."

On August 20th, Scott made his Dons debut in a 1-0 midweek win over Dumbarton at Boghead and just 10 days later, he returned to Dens Park, this time in the all-red strip of Aberdeen for the opening Premier League game. On an afternoon of blazing sunshine this was all a bit surreal for his previously adoring fans but two late goals from the home side ensured it was an unhappy return for Scott as his new club lost 3-2. "After so long with Dundee it was initially strange, especially returning to Dens Park so soon but I knew one or two of the Dons lads and soon settled," said Scott.

"When I signed for Aberdeen I became friendly with Drew Jarvie and Eddie Thomson. Eddie was a no-nonsense centre-half who didn't like strikers getting the better of him. Towards the end of his career, he moved to Australia, later moving into coaching there and ultimately doing well in a four-year spell as manager of their international team."

"Drew was a different type of character but, like Eddie, he hated to lose. Though normally a striker, he could also play in midfield and was just as likely to grab a goal coming from deep. We later defeated Rangers 5-1 in a League Cup semi-final and although I got a hat-trick Drew maintains that his goal was the pick of the bunch! But that is Drew and even now he remains highly competitive and it pains him to give me a 12-inch putt when we golf together!"

Jocky Scott would have more cause to celebrate in the next couple of clashes between Aberdeen and Dundee, scoring in a 2-0 win at Pittodrie and again in a 3-1 Ne-erday success at Dens Park but the Dons remained a pale shadow of the side that had done so well in the early 1970s. Stars like Martin Buchan, Joe Harper and ex-Dens Parker Steve Murray had gone, Eddie Turnbull himself had departed to manage Hibs and despite assistant-manager Jimmy Bonthrone stepping up, the Dons went into decline. Fans had drifted away and soon after Scott's arrival, the up and coming Scotland Under-23 international centre-half Willie Young also moved on, to Tottenham Hotspur for £100,000.

"That was a blow for Aberdeen but it was a traumatic time for big Willie who'd been one of the so called "Copenhagen Five" along with team-mate Arthur Graham, Joe Harper (Hibs), Pat McCluskey (Celtic), and Scotland captain Billy Bremner (Leeds United). All were given an SFA life ban following incidents after Scotland's 1-0 win over Denmark in the European Championships on September 3rd, though a year later, Graham and Harper had their bans lifted," recalled Scott.

"Soon afterwards, we were down to ten men when Joe Smith was sent off in game against Dundee United at Pittodrie. Two goals down with 20 minutes left, the manager brought on a striker, Billy Pirie, in place of Young. But, not best impressed, big Willie hurled his jersey into the dug-out, stormed up the tunnel and was off to Spurs a few days later!"

The slide continued and by October, the under-pressure Bonthrone had resigned to be replaced by Ayr United manager Ally McLeod. Even then, Aberdeen laboured and as the season moved into its final quarter, they went nine games without a win. The new Premier League had turned out to be something of a minefield and now no fewer than five clubs were in danger of joining struggling St Johnstone in dropping into the First Division.

Things looked grim for the Dons but in their final game, a 3-0 win against Hibs at Pittodrie ensured their Premier League survival on goal difference. In the end, Aberdeen finished alongside Dundee United and Dundee on 32 points but it was Dundee with a far inferior goal-difference, who took the drop. The Dons and United would go from strength to strength but it was the start of a major decline for the Dark Blues.

Davie White had indeed given youth a chance but a succession of injuries to key players had meant an over-reliance on the youngsters and the result had been clear. Scott, though, had done well at Pittodrie, finishing top scorer with 15 goals from 33 starting appearances, one goal more than erstwhile team-mate Gordon Wallace, who tellingly had netted more than twice as many of any of his Dens Park colleagues. In short, Scott's experience and scoring touch had been sorely missed and Aberdeen's gain was surely Dundee's loss.

Following their near escape, Dons boss Ally McLeod, himself an outstanding winger with Third Lanark, Hibs, Blackburn and Scotland, made a number of shrewd signings to ensure that there would be no repeat. In came Falkirk's attacking right-back Stuart Kennedy, right-winger Dom Sullivan was signed from Clyde, while the return of former Dons pin-up boy Joe Harper further rekindled the supporters' enthusiasm. "Joe Harper had been a prolific scorer in two spells with Morton, Huddersfield and Aberdeen before joining Everton for £180,000 in late 1972. Thirteen months later, he was re-united with Eddie Turnbull at Hibs but he struggled to win over the Easter Road support and was delighted to return to what he regarded as his spiritual home at Pittodrie," said Scott.

That meant there was fierce competition for the jerseys with Jocky Scott now vying with ex-Killie target man Ian Fleming, Drew Jarvie, Davie Robb and Joe Harper for a place up front. Aberdeen tended to play in a 4-3-3 formation with Scott, Robb or Jarvie dropping off the other two strikers and with the team gelling quickly, McLeod's men finished top of their League Cup section ahead of Ayr United, Kilmarnock and St Mirren. Dons' goal-machine Joe Harper had scored in every tie but although he managed another in the 1-0 quarter-final first-leg win over Stirling Albion at Pittodrie, their First Division opponents produced a shock 1-0 win at Annfield.

The scores remained locked after extra-time but, finding himself back on familiar territory in the Dens Park replay, Jocky Scott was on hand to knock in the opener as the Dons cruised into the last four by two goals to nil. Premier League Champions Rangers were the barrier to a place in the final but although there was the added handicap of having to play the tie in midweek in Glasgow, Aberdeen were neck and neck with Celtic and Dundee United at the top of the table and confidence was high.

It was to prove a glory night for Jocky Scott, who was so often a thorn in Ibrox club's side. Within two minutes, he smashed the ball past a despairing Stewart Kennedy after a lung-bursting run and cross by Dom Sullivan. Soon afterwards, he powered through for another and although Rangers reduced the leeway, the Dons number eight threaded a delightful through ball for

Harper to make it 3-1. Jarvie thundered home a fourth and worse was to come for the shell-shocked Light Blues when the irrepressible Scott clipped the ball in to complete his hat-trick after a clever free-kick routine.

That made it an astonishing 5-1 victory which Jocky Scott acknowledged was the game for which he would always be fondly remembered at Pittodrie. In an interview with Andy Melvin of the *Aberdeen Evening Express* he said: "I was chuffed to score a hat-trick on such a big occasion but the whole team played well. I was just lucky to be there to put away the chances. Rangers were not really bad last night but Aberdeen were brilliant. I've been a Dons player for a year now and I think that this was the best display yet. I know my form has been hot and cold since coming here but it really clicked for me last night." Melvin concluded: "It certainly did. This was the Jocky Scott that opposing defences all over Scotland fear. He fought to get into scoring positions then slotted the ball away making it look all too easy."

Ten days later, on November 6th, a huge support from the North-East descended on Hampden to swell the crowd for the League Cup Final against Celtic to 69,679. For a number of weeks the Dons, with regular left-back Chic McLelland injured and the recently signed Jim Shirra in midfield had been virtually unchanged. However, Shirra was cup-tied with Falkirk and Aberdeen fielded: *Clark; Kennedy, Gardner, Miller, Williamson; Sullivan, Smith, Graham; Jarvie, Harper, Scott. Subs. - Robb, Campbell. Celtic: Latchford: McGrain, Edvaldsson, MacDonald, Lynch; Doyle, Aitken, Burns; Glavin, Dalglish, Wilson. Subs. - Lennox, McCluskey.*

In the first minute Scott broke through only to shoot over and he was again prominent with a deflected shot. However, Celtic were not prepared to allow Aberdeen to play the expansive game that had destroyed Rangers and Scott's early promise was curtailed by a bad tackle by McGrain who was booked. Aberdeen had it all to do when Drew Jarvie was adjudged to have downed Kenny Dalgish in the box and the Celtic striker swept home the resultant penalty. That brought some niggly exchanges between Dalglish and Harper but, in 24 minutes, the stocky Dons striker unselfishly nodded a deep cross by Graham back across goal and Jarvie sent a powerful header into the net for the equaliser.

In the second half, Aberdeen were fortunate to survive some fierce attacks as the Parkhead side attacked incessantly but with Willie Gardner and skipper Willie Miller in inspirational form the Dons held firm. It appeared there could only be one winner but three minutes into extra-time, an isolated counter-attack ended with Davie Robb - a substitute for Jarvie - bundling the ball home to the delight of "Ally's Red Army" massed on the terraces behind that very goal at the "Rangers end" of the ground.

Celtic continued to attack frantically but it was Aberdeen's cup and that night there were widespread celebrations throughout the city with *The Green*

Final headlines reading: *"It's Magic - Robb is the Hampden Hero!"* Next day Aberdeen FC's official party, who had stopped overnight at a Perth hotel for a celebration banquet, returned to the Granite City as Jocky Scott, now the proud holder of League Cup winners' medals for both Aberdeen and Dundee, recalled: "It was a thrilling, hard-fought victory against a very good Celtic team and when we paraded the Cup we got a great reception with tens of thousands of people lining the streets and filling Pittodrie itself."

"Although we beat both of the Old Firm to win the League Cup, some wondered why we did so well against Rangers, yet were pushed back on the defensive for so long by Celtic," said Scott. "The answer, possibly, is that without a midfield battler like Jim Shirra, who'd done really well in the recent 2-1 league win over Celtic at Pittodrie but was cup-tied, we had a very attacking midfield. On the night, it all came off against Rangers, whereas forewarned, Celtic who took a very tough approach were maybe better prepared to deal with us."

Scott recalled the decisive moments: "The running power of Arthur Graham caused Celtic no end of problems. His right-wing cross created our first goal and in extra-time he made a great cross-field run from the left, dragging Danny McGrain across the park, before passing to me out on the right. I crossed hard and low across the edge of the box but Arthur who was looking for the return, miscued, completely wrong-footing the Celtic defence as well as Joe Harper and the ball skidded on towards the far post where Davie Robb ran in to hit it in off the chest of Celtic keeper Peter Latchford!"

"That was a fantastic moment and rather bizarre too, for at breakfast that morning at our Glasgow hotel, goalkeeper Bobby Clark, who was Davie Robb's room-mate, told us he'd dreamt that Robb would come off the bench and score! Davie was a fierce competitor and a great servant in his dozen years or so at Pittodrie. He was popular with the fans and they affectionately nicknamed him "The Brush" due to his bushy red hair and his perceived resemblance to cartoon character Basil Brush."

"Both of us had been on the Chelsea ground staff as youngsters and I met him again while on tour with Scotland in 1971. We were born within a month of each other in the late 1940's and while he was from Broughty Ferry and was a Dundee fan who joined Aberdeen, I was from Aberdeen and grew up following the Dons before signing for Dundee!"

At the end of that season, Arthur Graham went south to Leeds and later played for Manchester United and Bradford City, as well as making 11 Scotland appearances. Willie Miller, of course, made an Aberdeen record of well over 500 appearances and captained the club to an astonishing 12 trophy successes as well as turning out for Scotland on 65 occasions. Legendary Aberdeen manager Alex Ferguson, who would take charge of the Scots in 1978, described Miller as "the best penalty-box defender in the

World" but at that time there was no more popular player than Joe Harper, who was nicknamed "King Joey" by his adoring fans.

Harper was a natural goal-scorer, a real personality on and off the park who went on to set a Dons record of 205 competitive goals as Scott confirmed: "I had the pleasure of playing alongside Joe Harper who was a deadly striker. He was renowned for his goal-scoring but was far more than that. He had great ability when in possession and was an excellent passer of the ball as well. However, it was his scoring ability that brought him to everyone's attention and his quickness of mind and feet in a crowded goalmouth brought him many goals. He did not have a naturally athletic physique but was very stocky with a similar build to another great striker, Gerd Muller of West Germany. But he was powerful and fast over a short distance and like Muller absolutely lethal anywhere near goal."

However, according to Scott, there was no greater character than Ally McLeod, who had George Murray as his coach and Ronnie Coutts as the physiotherapist: "We used to play small-sided games in the ash car park opposite Pittodrie's main stand and Ally was forever winding up former Scotland goalkeeper Bobby Clark. There were often restrictions like playing with two-touches, only being allowed to pass the ball forward, or using just your left foot but basically Ally just pleased himself."

"One time with his team losing heavily, he announced that the next goal would be worth five goals. Ally then took a shot at goal - two small posts stuck in the ground - and although clearly miles over, he declared that it was the winner. Bobby Clark, who took these affairs seriously, was none too impressed and stormed off in the huff much to Ally's delight! Ally, however, made a number of excellent signings for the club. He was a great motivator and in my opinion he laid the foundations for a successful and ever-improving Aberdeen side that won the League Cup and went on to win so many other trophies under Alex Ferguson," he said.

In the league, Aberdeen went on to finish a creditable third behind the Old Firm with Scott starting 22 games and managing 14 goals. A year earlier, his great friend Gordon Wallace had gone to the USA to spend the summer playing for Seattle Sounders in the NASL – the North American Soccer League, and now had recommended Scott: "I was 29-years old at the time and jumped at the chance to sample football in America. There were some big names playing in the States at the time so I signed from May to the end of the NASL season in September."

Immediately the Scottish season ended, Jocky, his wife Elaine and their three children Nicola (7), Jayson (5), and Ashley (3), flew to Seattle, a city with a 1.5 million population, in Washington State on the North-West coast of America near the Canadian border. Scott remembered the experience fondly: "It was a huge adventure for us all, while Nicola and Jayson were

A young John Scott, third left, in the thick of the action in this Aberdeen Primary Schools Cup Final at Pittodrie.

The smiling youngster is all ready for action for his Abbotswell Primary School team.

Chelsea manager Tommy Docherty shows his "keepy-uppy" skills watched by Phillip Mallard, Stuart Henderson, John Scott and another unidentified youth player at the Stamford Bridge club's Hendon training ground in 1963.

Teenage trio John Scott, Alex Totten and John Phillips made their debuts in a 6-0 victory over Motherwell in August 1964. Fotopress

Bob Shankly set the young Scott on the road to stardom.

The Dens starlet looks on top of the world as he leaps a crush barrier beneath the main stand. Fotopress

A youthful Scott enjoys tea as a guest of Andy Penman and wife Sandra who took him under their wing in his early days at Dens Park. DC Thomson

Dundee FC 1965-66 (Back, left to right) George Ryden, Jim Easton, Davie Duncan, Ally Donaldson, Willie Law, Steve Murray, Alex Kinninmonth. Middle - Bobby Seith (coach), Davie Swan, Alex Stuart, Tom Weir, Doug Houston, Norrie Beattie, Charlie Cooke, George Stewart. Front - Andy Penman, Hugh Reid, Alex Hamilton, Tony Harvey, Alan Cousin, Jocky Scott, Kenny Cameron.

Derby delight for Scott - by then it was Jocky - after the grounded Andy Penman has scored for Dundee in a 1-1 draw with Dundee United at Dens Park. Dave Martin Fotopress

Jocky Scott blasts home against Rangers then takes the cheers with George McLean at Dens Park in 1968.

The Dens buzz-bomb gives Manchester United defender Tony Dunne a tough time in a 4-2 tour triumph in San Francisco.

Signing for life - Jocky Scott with wife Elaine on their wedding day in Dundee in 1969.

Jocky's on the ball again in this picture-perfect pose at Dens Park in 1970. Gordon Gurvan

Dundee FC 1968-69 with Jocky an established first-team player. Back row - Bobby Wilson, Steve Murray, Ally Donaldson, Jim Easton, Doug Houston, Davie Swan. Front - Billy Campbell, Jocky Scott, Joe Gilroy, Alex Kinninmonth, Alex Bryce. Fotopress

Jocky Scott beats Celtic's Jim Brogan in the 1970 Scottish Cup semi-final at Hampden Park. Scott rated the hard-tackling Brogan his most difficult opponent.   DC Thomson

Jocky Scott fires home from the penalty spot against Hamish McAlpine in the 6-4 derby win over Dundee United in 1971.

Dundee FC 1971-72 - (back row) Bobby Wilson, Iain Phillip, Mike Hewitt, Ally Donaldson, George Stewart, Dave Johnston, Jim McLean (coach). Middle - John Prentice (manager), Bobby Robinson, Ian Scott, Jim Steele, Ron Selway, Duncan Lambie, Maurice Friel (physio). Front - Alex Bryce, John Duncan, Alex Kinninmonth, Doug Houston, Gordon Wallace, Jocky Scott, Jimmy Wilson.

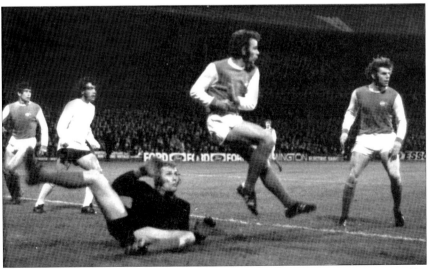

Frantic goalmouth action from the 1971 UEFA Cup tie against Cologne which Scott described as his most exciting game when Dundee overcame the West Germans 5-4 on aggregate. DC Thomson

A grinning Jocky Scott introduces new coach Harold Davis to (from left) Bobby Wilson, Dave Johnston, Gordon Wallace, Mike Hewitt, Dave Soutar, Harold Davis, Jocky Scott, Doug Houston, Bobby Ford, Jimmy Wilson, Alex Kinninmonth, John Duncan

Smiles from Doug Houston, Iain Phillip, John Duncan, Thomson Allan, Andy Penman, Bobby Robinson, Ian Scott, Jocky Scott, Bobby Wilson, Gordon Wallace, George Stewart and Alan Gilzean after a Testimonial for United's Dennis Gillespie in 1973.

Jocky Scott nets against Dunfermline at East End Park to put Dundee on their way towards League Cup glory in 1973.

This time Jocky shoots past the RWD Molenbeek keeper in a UEFA Cup tie at Dens in 1974 - his only goal in European competition.

Jocky's joy as Gordon Wallace gives Dundee a 1-0 win over Celtic in the 1973 League Cup Final.

Glory day as Dundee return with the League Cup. Jubilant fans cheer their heroes as Gordon Wallace raises the trophy alongside team-mates George Stewart and Bobby Ford. DC Thomson

A joyous celebration ensued at Dundee's Angus Hotel. Back - Jocky Scott, Bobby Wilson, Duncan Lambie, Jimmy Wilson, John Duncan, Gordon Wallace, Iain Phillip, Dave Johnston, Eric Ferguson (physio), Tom Arnott (chief scout), Ian Scott, Jimmy Toner (coach), George Stewart, Hugh Robertson (coach), Bobby Ford. Front - unknown, Tommy Gemmell, Lord Provost Tom Moore, Davie White (manager), Harry Davis (coach). Inset Bobby Robinson and Thomson Allan. DCThomson

Dens Park hot-shots Jocky Scott, John Duncan and Gordon Wallace get the travelling trunk ready in 1974. Stephen Borland

Jocky Scott shoots past Jim McArthur of Hibs in the thrill-a-minute Scottish Cup tie which ended 3-3 at Easter Road in 1974.

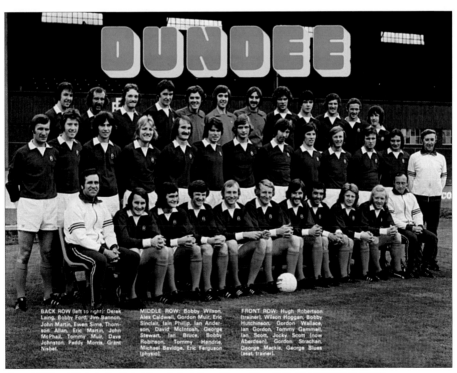

BACK ROW (left to right): Derek Laing, Bobby Ford, Jim Bannon, John Martin, Ewen Sime, Thomson Allan, Eric Martin, John McPhail, Tommy Muir, Dave Johnston, Paddy Morris, Grant Nisbet. MIDDLE ROW: Bobby Wilson, Alex Caldwell, Gordon Muir, Eric Sinclair, Iain Phillip, Ian Anderson, David McIntosh, George Stewart, Ian Bruce, Bobby Robinson, Tommy Hendrie, Michael Bavidge, Eric Ferguson (physio). FRONT ROW: Hugh Robertson (trainer), Wilson Hoggan, Bobby Hutchinson, Gordon Wallace, Ian Gordon, Tommy Gemmell, Ian Scott, Jocky Scott (now Aberdeen), Gordon Strachan, George Mackie, George Blues (asst. trainer).

August 1975 and it's Jocky Scott's last Dens Park photo-call for a while with Gordon Strachan on his left.

Now a Don (left), Scott looks a dedicated follower of fashion as he meets new team-mates Willie Young, Eddie Thomson and Billy Pirie.

Dons dangerman Jocky Scott lurks with intent as Dundee United goalkeeper Hamish McAlpine claws the ball away with Alan Forsyth an onlooker in a 3-2 Aberdeen win at Pittodrie.

League Cup glory for the Dons and Jocky Scott as Davie Robb arrives at the back post to ram the ball past Celtic keeper Peter Latchford for the winner in October 1976.   DC Thomson

Aberdeen's 1976 League Cup winning squad (back, left to right) Jocky Scott, Joe Harper, Dom Sullivan, Willie Miller, Stuart Kennedy, Chic McClelland, Drew Jarvie, Arthur Graham. Front - Davie Robb, Willie Gardner, Joe Smith, Bobby Clark, Eddie Thomson, Billy Williamson, Ian Fleming.

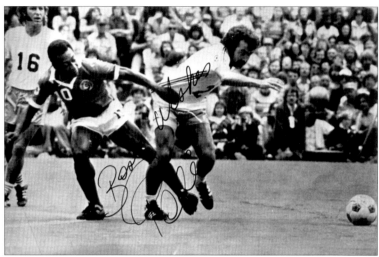

Jocky Scott tussles with Pele in an NASL match between Seattle Sounders and New York Cosmos in the mid-70s. This photo was autographed by the Brazilian who was long regarded as the world's greatest player.

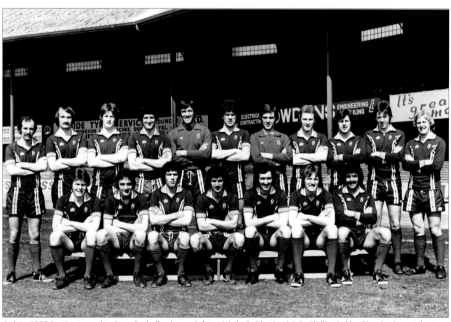

In late 1977 Scott returned to Dens Park. (back row, left to right) - Bobby Ford, Iain Phillip, Bobby Glennie, Dave Johnston, Ally Donaldson, John McPhail, Thomson Allan, George McGeachie, Ian McDougall, Alex Caldwell, Jim Shirra. Front - Dave McKinnon, Ian Redford, Erich Schaedler, Billy Pirie, Billy Williamson, Eric Sinclair, Jocky Scott. DC Thomson also expected to attend school. We loved the lifestyle and settled easily enough as all the British players lived in the same apartment block which of course had the obligatory swimming pool!"

Seattle played their home games at a huge indoor, all-seated stadium called the Kingdome which was also used for motor racing, baseball, basketball, circuses, rodeos, political rallies, and religious crusades and boasted a 3,000 square foot TV screen which provided instant replays. Its capacity for football was 65,000 though the evangelist Billy Graham had attracted a then record attendance of 73,000.

Sounders' manager was a familiar name, none other than ex-Dundee, Everton and Scotland half-back Jimmy Gabriel. Wallace and Scott had been recommended by a Broughty Ferry friend of his father, Jimmy Johnstone. Prior to Scott's arrival, Sounders had struggled but he made an immediate impact by heading the winner against the famous New York Cosmos. That began the run that propelled Seattle towards the Soccer Bowl Final and another memorable moment involved him netting another decisive goal against the equally famous Los Angeles Aztecs, who featured former Manchester United and Northern Ireland great, George Best.

"As well as Gordon Wallace and former St Mirren and 'Spurs winger Jimmy Robertson, there was England international Mike England, also ex-Tottenham Hotspur, and the following season the legendary West Ham United and England International Bobby Moore arrived. Moore, who had captained his country to World Cup glory in 1966, was still a great player, very modest and a thoroughly decent man. There were others that I knew playing for other teams like former Aberdeen team-mates Davie Robb, Eddie Thomson and Bobby Clark."

"The standard was very high with many top players in the NASL at the time. I played against the great Pele three times, and although in the twilight of his career, he was still the best I ever came up against. As well as him, there were other top stars like of course George Best, 1970 Brazil World Cup winning captain Carlos Alberto, Franz Beckenbauer, who lifted the World Cup for West Germany in 1974, Johann Cruyff and many more."

In the final, Seattle again played New York Cosmos, who, as well as Pele, Carlos Alberto and Beckenbauer, had other World Cup stars in Italian striker Georgio Chinaglia and West Germany's Franz Roth. "We lost 2-1 but the whole thing was a wonderful experience," said Scott. "Many of the games were played on Astroturf which I really enjoyed and when we reached the Soccer Bowl Final, our average attendance was around 26,000."

It was September before Jocky Scott returned to Pittodrie from America but by then Ally McLeod had departed to take charge of the Scotland international team that would go on to play in the World Cup Finals the following year. Former Celtic captain Billy McNeill, the first British player to lift the European Cup in 1967, was the new manager. He had only been in charge of Clyde since April but he was a man of some stature and had done enough to persuade the Aberdeen board of directors that he was the man for the vacant post at Pittodrie.

By the time of Scott's return, the '77/78 season was six or seven games old. Clearly the new boss wanted to build his own side and with the pacy Duncan Davidson starting to make his mark and tricky Dundee midfielder Gordon Strachan signed in exchange for Jim Shirra plus £50,000 in late October, the writing was on the wall. Initially, Scott rejected the opportunity to return south as part of the Strachan deal but, desperate to return to first-team action and with new Dens boss Tommy Gemmell still keen, the Aberdonian finally rejoined the Dark Blues a few weeks later for a fee of around £15,000.

Later in his Dundee v Aberdeen Testimonial Programme of 1981, Scott looked back fondly on his time at Pittodrie: "I loved almost every minute of it because something was always happening. In general the fans were good to me, though sometimes I felt that because I was a local boy they were a bit more critical than supporters at Dundee. Jimmy Bonthrone was one of the best-liked men in football and a fine coach. But he was too nice a man to be a football manager. Jimmy was better as a buffer between manager and players. Ally McLeod was all about motivation and enthusiasm and those qualities ended a lean spell for the club. I was only under Billy McNeill for a short spell. Even so, you could see his organisation was tremendous and he was also very good on tactics."

"I wish I'd been able to stay there a bit longer, but it just wasn't to be. I'll always treasure that period as one of the highlights in my career. Apart from my League Cup medal, there were other less obvious benefits. I gained enormous experience from working under such a variety of managers at such a progressive club. I was also privileged to play alongside some marvellous players like Joe Harper, Drew Jarvie, Arthur Graham, Bobby Clark and a budding youngster called Willie Miller. I only hope I get the chance to utilise that experience if I ever become a manager in my own right."

That, though was all for the future.

Chapter 8

A Dens Return

Jocky Scott's return to Dens Park came as a welcome boost to a Dundee support desperate for promotion to the Premier League. The appointment of former skipper Tommy Gemmell as manager in place of Davie White for the 1977-78 season had brought a new, refreshing approach and despite losing the highly talented Gordon Strachan, supporters got a major boost from the arrival of experienced campaigners like Scott and Jim Shirra from Aberdeen, as well as Hibernian left-back Eric Schaedler.

Most of the Dundee players were well known to Scott, while he was also well acquainted with Billy Pirie, Billy Williamson, Jim Shirra and the soon to arrive Bobby Glennie from his time at Aberdeen. "I was glad to return to Dens and felt that there was a group of players who were well capable of getting Dundee back up. Shirra was a highly competitive midfielder who impressed me with the Dons, Schaedler a hard-tackling defender who'd been capped for Scotland in 1974, while I regarded Pirie as a natural goal-scorer after playing alongside him at Pittodrie," explained Scott.

"Billy, in fact, was a prolific scorer for Huntly in the Highland League then at Arbroath in the old Division One. For some reason, it didn't work out for him at Aberdeen but in his first season with Dundee he got 44 goals and continued to bang them in after I arrived too. Just like Joe Harper at Pittodrie, Pirie became something of a cult hero with the Dens fans; Billy Williamson netted a lot of goals as an attacking midfielder and Bobby Glennie - a lifelong Dundee fan - would prove a defensive stalwart over the next decade or so."

By then almost 30 years of age, Jocky Scott was handed a deeper, more creative role just behind the main strike-force of Billy Pirie and Eric Sinclair or the fast-emerging Ian Redford. Scott's return against Hamilton at Dens attracted a crowd of nearly 7,000 - about 1,000 more than usual - and although he didn't score, his composure and use of the ball was evident as the Dark Blues raced to a three-nil win.

"Just seven months earlier, I'd been in the Dons side that lost to Dundee in the Scottish Cup quarter-final replay at Pittodrie. They'd played really well and it was their misfortune to lose out on promotion to Alex Ferguson's St Mirren who had stars like Tony Fitzpatrick, Billy Stark and Frank McGarvey, and Clydebank who featured the great Davie Cooper. It was no easier when I arrived either for we faced fierce competition from Morton and relegated Hearts," observed Scott. "Like Clydebank, Morton were very much a good team but just as the Bankies had "Super Cooper", they had a superbly gifted individual in big Andy Ritchie who got them a pile of goals."

"Nevertheless, by Christmas we were top of the league and there were crowds of well over 12,000 at Dens Park for the games against Morton and St Johnstone. These were incredible gates for the lower league even though they were dwarfed by a First Division record attendance of 19,720 - including a huge support from Dundee - when we met Hearts at Tynecastle in early January 1978."

"Thomson Allan, Dave McKinnon and Dave Johnston were left out after we'd lost 4-3 to St Johnstone five days earlier and the teams were: *Hearts - Dunlop; Kidd, McNicoll, Tierney, Jefferies; Bannon, Fraser, Prentice; Shaw, Busby, Gibson. Subs. - Brown, Rodger. Dundee - Donaldson; Turnbull, Caldwell, McPhail, Schaedler; Shirra, McDougall, Williamson; Sinclair, Pirie, Scott. Subs. - McKinnon, Redford.*"

"That ended two apiece but although we kept racking up the points and were back on top towards the end of March, we just couldn't shake off Hearts and Morton. Attack was the name of the game under Gemmell but we blew it in a four-day spell in April, only managing a draw in a crucial clash with Morton at Dens before losing 2-1 at Dumbarton a few days later," said Scott.

"The Boghead reverse was a sore one - myself, Jim Shirra and Ian McDougall were dropped - and that result was to cost us the league. For despite taking full points from our last three games including a 3-2 win at Cappielow on the final day, Morton were promoted as champions along with Hearts who got a last-minute winner at Arbroath. Dundee were just a point behind them both so if we'd taken even a point at Boghead, we would have gone up with a better goal difference," concluded Scott.

It had been expected that the former Scotland international, who had enjoyed a virtually injury-free career, would play a key role in the promotion run-in. However, in February, Scott began to experience pains down his leg which affected his back and despite a seemingly successful series of manipulations under anaesthetic, the pain refused to subside: "I continued to play until the last few games although it was a struggle at times."

That summer, all of Scotland's attention was focussed on the national team's performances in the 1978 World Cup Finals in Argentina. But by then, Scott was back in the United States as he recalled: "I'd recovered sufficiently to play for Seattle but the problems continued and after a couple of substitute appearances for Dundee in August, I was prescribed complete rest. Two days before Christmas, I returned to the starting line-up against Airdrie at Broomfield but although we won 2-0, I suffered a recurrence and it was back to the specialist."

Scott was referred to an Aberdeen neurosurgeon, whose diagnosis of a trapped nerve entailed the player undergoing surgery at Strathcathro Hospital where it was found that two discs rather than one were causing the pain. "I was told the injury was down to wear and tear and that the constant twisting and turning down the years had taken its toll," said Scott. By the time I recovered, I'd been out of the game for the best part of a year and although I returned to reserve-team football, I began to consider my future."

"By then, it was early 1980 but although I still had a contract at Dens, I was no longer able to do any real training and actually applied for a couple of jobs outside football. I had no success but then came news that Willie Wallace, first-team coach and effectively Gemmell's assistant, had opted for a new life in Australia to became manager of Apia in Sydney. Hugh Robertson, who had been a coach at Dens with first-team and reserves since 1973, took his place and soon afterwards an advert for the position of reserve-team coach appeared in the local newspaper. I applied, spoke to Tommy Gemmell and a few days later he confirmed that the post was mine until the end of the season!"

Jocky Scott the player was now Jocky Scott the coach although he felt somewhat apprehensive in taking charge of his early coaching sessions: "Initially, I did little routines that I'd enjoyed as a player but in reality they had little to do with what the players really needed to work on. And it was only when I started to take my coaching badges at Largs that I managed to get a better insight into things and become more focussed."

Tommy Gemmell, meanwhile, had led Dundee to the First Division Championship and promotion in '78/79 but having sacrificed skill for graft to get the team up, the Dark Blues lacked the quality to survive in the Premier League. And having spent three years outwith the top flight and lacking the financial means to bring in better players, relegation followed a season of struggle and Gemmell was dismissed.

His replacement for the approaching 1980-81 season was former Dundee United goalkeeper Donald Mackay, who, more recently had been manager of Norresundby Boldklub in Denmark. By then, Scott felt fully recovered from his troublesome back injury and targeted a first-team return while continuing to coach the reserves. Keen to have such an influential performer back in the side, Mackay was happy to give him his chance but after just five first-team appearances, the Dens veteran realised the worst: "The old sharpness had gone. I felt I could no longer attain my previous standard and my comeback didn't last long! Sadly, it was time to hang up my boots but I looked forward to concentrating on my coaching career."

"Perhaps fittingly, my last game was at Dens Park against Hibs, who had also been relegated. Playing for them was none other than George Best, the former Manchester United star who I'd last played against when he was with Los Angeles Aztecs in the USA. He had signed for Hibs the previous November and was on £2,000 a game - not bad money if you could get it back then! Hibs reaped the benefit with bumper gates but although the flashes of genius remained, "Bestie" was past his best and couldn't prevent them going down. At the time, he was 34, a couple of years older than me, and after just a few more appearances, he returned to play in the USA."

At this time Dundee FC were in grave danger of becoming the perennial "yo-yo" club - too good for the First Division but never good enough to remain in the Premier League. In those circumstances, Donald Mackay did very well, taking the club to the League Cup Final - played at Dens Park rather than Tannadice on the toss of a coin - which they lost 3-0 to Dundee United, but, far more importantly, guiding them back to the Premier League and consolidating their position over the following two and a half years. Alongside him was new first-team coach Frank Upton, a strict disciplinarian, who had been a senior Chelsea player in Scott's short spell at Stamford Bridge in 1963-64 and a coach at Aston Villa and Chelsea.

Upton's arrival meant a step back for Hugh Robertson, and despite the Englishman's imminent departure to manage Al Arabi in Kuwait, Robertson was released for "financial reasons" immediately after Dundee's promotion was confirmed in May 1981. Bristol City head coach Ken Wimhurst, who Mackay knew from his own time as a youth coach at Ashton Gate, replaced Upton but when he in turn resigned in November 1982, Scott, who had diligently continued to hone his coaching skills, was given the opportunity to become first-team coach.

"I was really pleased to take that step and very fortunate to have worked and learned from such a variety of managers and coaches at Dens Park. Upton and Mackay had both worked in Denmark, while Mackay and Wimhurst had both been with Bristol City in the English First Division," said Scott. "Shug Robertson had had a great career as a player at Dundee, Dunfermline and Arbroath before joining the coaching staff at Dens in 1973. He was a great help to me both as a player and as a coach and it was no surprise to read that Gordon Strachan was full of praise for Shug and what he added to his game."

"As I've said earlier, Bob Seith and Jim McLean were a big influence, while, by then, I'd played or coached under no fewer than six Dundee managers - excluding Sammy Kean who was interim - Bob Shankly, Bobby Ancell, John Prentice, Davie White, Tommy Gemmell and Don Mackay, who all contributed to my development in their own unique way. Shankly knew the game inside-out and kind of frightened you into doing your best but I've got to say McLean was the best coach I had - his knowledge, training and his drive to get the best out of you really worked for me. "

"In recent years, I'd taken a keen interest in the development of our younger players. Jim McLean and Dundee United were deservedly praised for the young talent they produced and their achievements in the late '70s and '80s but we also had talented youngsters coming through. Our relegation from the initial Premier League and subsequent failure to get out of the First

Division set us back badly as a club but Gordon Strachan was a brilliant prospect here before joining Aberdeen, while my move into coaching came shortly before Ian Redford's transfer to Rangers for a Scottish record fee of £210,000," said Scott.

"Ian was a talented striker who'd blossomed in the Premier League but his departure gave 17-year-old Iain Ferguson the chance to make his mark. That he did in spectacular style, netting twice in Dundee's 5-1 victory over Celtic at Dens Park, a result which didn't keep Dundee up but cost Billy McNeill's team the title to Aberdeen in 1980."

"Stewart McKimmie, a superb all-round defender and the more attack-minded Tosh McKinlay were top-class full-backs and after leaving us - McKimmie to Aberdeen for £90,000 in 1983, McKinlay to Hearts for £300,000 in 1988 - both went on to become full Scotland internationals. Ray Stephen gave us a lot of energy up front as well as getting the goals. He was a great guy to have around while Rab Shannon was another Scotland Under-21 international who came through our ranks, a versatile player - either at full-back or midfield - and a real unsung hero."

However, danger was never far away in the Premier League and, following a disappointing run of results, Donald Mackay was forced to resign in December 1983. By then, Jocky Scott felt confident enough to apply for the vacant post: "I felt I'd done well with the reserves and had enough experience to handle the job but, instead, Archie Knox, who had been Alex Ferguson's assistant-manager at Aberdeen for three years, got the nod. I was very disappointed but, to be honest, the directors did me a huge favour in appointing Archie as I was to learn so much working with him."

The new manager had visited Scott's Broughty Ferry home to reassure Scott that he wanted him as his right-hand man. This was a gesture much appreciated with the Aberdonian thereafter content to serve a hands-on apprenticeship alongside the battle-hardened Knox, who had earlier had a successful four-year spell as manager of Forfar Athletic. "Archie really was a huge influence on me and it's true that he could be really hard on the players. But that was only because he recognised that they could do better, and he was determined that each individual would play to his capacity in every game," said Scott.

In the next few months, Knox and Scott led the Dark Blues to the Scottish Cup semi-final, having defeated Rangers in a thrilling quarter-final replay at Ibrox. Disappointingly, they lost 2-0 to Aberdeen and a series of poor league results meant a tension-fraught end to the '83/84 campaign. It took a point in the penultimate game against Hearts to consign St Johnstone to the drop along with Motherwell and later a relieved Scott revealed: "We drew 1-1 with a very good Hearts side but if we'd lost, a defeat in the final match against Saints at Dens would've meant them staying up and us going down.

Our plans for the club would have been in ruins but although it was nervy stuff in Gorgie that night, we held on and could start to look ahead."

"Enthusiasm was high amongst the support and over the next two seasons, we managed to get Dundee up to a higher level of performance and rather than constantly looking over our shoulders, we could realistically aim for a European spot. Firstly, though, we had to replace our skipper and inspirational midfielder Cammy Fraser, Iain Ferguson who'd scored 50 goals in three seasons and Jim McInally who'd been an excellent holding midfielder while on loan from Celtic. Unfortunately, McInally was sold to Nottingham Forest who'd offered more than us, while the other two joined Rangers on freedom of contract with Dundee later getting £350,000 in compensation."

"Archie, though, knew just who he wanted and moved quickly to bring in John Brown from Hamilton, Robert Connor from Ayr United and Stuart Rafferty from Motherwell. All were midfielders and cost us a total of £115,000, which was really good business as it turned out. To stiffen the defence we got John McCormack, a big no-nonsense centre-half, from St Mirren in an exchange deal with Dumbarton's Tom Carson signed to provide competition for Bobby Geddes in goal."

"We had some great games at that time and several spring to mind. We won 4-3 against United at Tannadice in something of a classic. Three times we went ahead only for United to equalise, but, late on, John Brown popped up to head the winner. Dundee played in a very positive way under Knox - there was a tremendous fighting spirit and no little skill - and having defeated Rangers 3-2 to get to the last four of the Scottish Cup the previous year, we again beat them in the cup at Ibrox in '84/85, only narrowly losing out to Celtic after a replay in the following round. That season, we came close to a European place, winning five out of our last six games but there was no slip-up from St Mirren, so it didn't quite happen."

"Archie strengthened the team by paying £65,000 for Morton central-defender Jim Duffy, who, arguably, was every bit as good as Aberdeen's Willie Miller and Dave Narey of Dundee United. If Duff hadn't got injured, I think we might just have picked up some silverware and he might well have made the full Scotland team. Anyway, '85/86 was another good season and we were again in contention for the last UEFA Cup spot, this time with Rangers who had recently brought in Graeme Souness as their player-manager. In our final game on Saturday, May 3rd, we had to beat Hearts at Dens Park and hope Motherwell might do something against them at Ibrox."

"It was an even bigger game for Hearts, who were unbeaten in 29 games and held a two-point lead over Celtic. They needed just a point to ensure their first championship success since 1960 but having witnessed Dundee United win the title at Dens Park three years earlier, there was no way we wished to endure a similar experience. With just seven minutes left there was no scoring and Archie decided to go for broke by replacing left-back Tosh McKinlay with an attacking midfielder, Albert Kidd."

"Now Albert was a very good player who'd been at Dens for five years but, although on occasion he was brilliant, he was all too often inconsistent. That afternoon, though, he was brilliant, finding the net twice to shatter Hearts, whose title dreams died as news filtered through that Celtic had beaten St Mirren 5-0 to win the league on goal difference. The same rule thwarted us for despite an earlier rumour that Motherwell had scored a late winner, it was later confirmed that Rangers had won 2-0 to pip us on goal-difference which made for a sombre post-match atmosphere in both home and away dressing rooms that fateful afternoon."

Chapter 9

Scott in Charge

Just four weeks later, Archie Knox was again in the thick of the action, this time at the 1986 World Cup Finals in Mexico as assistant to Alex Ferguson, who was interim manager of the Scotland international team after Jock Stein's death nine months earlier. It was the fourth successive time the Scots had qualified for the finals but despite appearing to have a decent chance of qualifying from a group including West Germany, Denmark and Uruguay, they were again eliminated after the initial group stages.

Jocky Scott, meanwhile, was also in North America, in charge of Dundee's three-week tour of the USA and Canada: "It was a fantastic trip - to the American states of California, Oregon and Washington in the west, then Florida in the east after visiting Alberta in Canada. We played 10 matches, mostly against local clubs like LA Heat, San Jose Earthquakes, Seattle Storm and the quaintly-named Edmonton Brick Men but we also fitted in a couple of friendlies against Manchester City - in San Jose - and Queens Park Rangers in Orlando. We drew with the two English sides - we'd only recently played City in Bobby Glennie's testimonial game at Dens Park - and won most of the others but it was clear that the standard of American football, or soccer as they prefer to call it, was markedly improved from my first visit 19 years earlier."

Within days of Scott's return to Scotland, however, came news that Knox had resigned in order to rejoin Aberdeen as co-manager alongside Alex Ferguson. That was a blow as Dundee had made great progress under Knox and Scott and the feeling had been that the only way was up. However, Scott had impressed in his role as assistant-manager and the Dens Park board acted decisively in appointing him as their new manager. By then, he had served the club for around 20 years - six and a half as coach or assistant-manager - and most supporters thought it only right that he should get his chance in the Dens Park hot seat.

"I was as disappointed as anyone when Archie decided to leave but was obviously delighted when I was appointed manager. I had waited a long time to be my own man but to cut my managerial teeth at a club of Dundee's standing was truly exciting and I couldn't wait to get started," said the new Dens boss, whose first move was to appoint his former Dons team-mate, Drew Jarvie, then a well-respected coach at St Mirren, as his assistant.

"It was a relatively seamless transition as I'd been working with the players for so long. Anyway, one thing I'd learned was that you had to have discipline around the place. Things were somewhat lax under Tommy Gemmell and Willie Wallace, and when the club parted company with

Donald Mackay, Donald himself later revealed in an interview with *The Scotsman* that chairman Ian Gellatly had told him he should be running some club's youth development as he was quite incapable of handling the senior players! That was harsh as Don had done a good job for the club but although there were indeed problems, Archie soon showed who was boss and woe betide anyone who challenged his authority!"

Over the past few years Dundee had built a really good side and the feeling was that they were only a couple of players away from breaking into the top four and making a real challenge at the top. But far from adding to his team, Jocky Scott had to endure the enforced sale of two of his top players as well as losing out on a prime transfer target - all within the first few months of the season - due to Dundee's deteriorating financial situation which saw debts escalate to around £600,000.

"The first player to go was Robert Connor, who'd recently gained his first full Scotland international cap against Holland. He rejoined Archie Knox at Aberdeen with Dundee getting £225,000 and Ian Angus in exchange. It might just as easily have been John Brown who was set to go to Hearts in a deal worth £300,000 with Andy Watson coming our way before it fell through due a failed medical. In November, Ray Stephen was also sold - for £150,000 to the French club Nancy - and in another setback we had lost out to Dundee United in our attempt to bring back Iain Ferguson from Rangers."

"Fergie had fallen out of favour and was happy to return to us on a year-long loan. He still had an eye for goal, netting twice in wins over St Mirren and Hibs but, unfortunately, Jim McLean stepped in, offered to buy him outright and he was recalled to Ibrox. We offered £100,000 but couldn't match their bid which was £40,000 higher, so, as you can imagine, I was gutted at our deal being hijacked. Ten years later, after spells at United, Hearts, Motherwell and Airdrie, he returned and insisted that he had desperately wanted to come here rather than cross the road back in 1986."

"Despite that, we made a decent start in the league and had a good run in the Skol-sponsored League Cup before losing 3-1 to Rangers in the quarter-final at Ibrox. Rangers, who had Scots of the calibre of Davie Cooper, Ally McCoist and Dave McPherson had raised the bar by signing England internationalists like Chris Woods and Terry Butcher, while Graeme Souness himself was a Scottish international midfielder of vast experience. So it was no disgrace to lose, especially as it had been 1-1 after the regulation 90 minutes and we'd had our centre-half Jim Smith ordered off after just half an hour of a tie that went to extra-time!"

"However, we had a good record against Rangers back then and got our revenge by beating them 1-0 at Dens soon afterwards. In contrast Dundee had often struggled against Dundee United in the same period but we managed to put one over them at Tannadice just a few days before Ray

Stephen departed for France," smiled Scott. "We knew that United liked to pull their two wide men deep. That left you to decide whether to go tight and risk the ball over the top or stay off them and suffer the consequences of allowing them space to collect the ball and create problems."

"We decided on a 3-5-2 formation, pushing our full-backs up tight on their wingers, while man-marking their strikers with a sweeper at the back to counter the ball over the top. It worked a treat and with an extra man in midfield we dominated the game. We wanted to get the ball in to Graeme Harvey's feet as he was great at holding the ball up and allowing players to link up. Everything came off for us with Harvey scoring two and Rab Shannon the other in a well-merited 3-0 win. It was the first time I'd tasted derby success as a manager and it was a real moment to savour."

Stephen's departure left Dundee short up front but the Dundee manager was to make a couple of inspired signings. In came Dundee United striker Tommy Coyne (24), for £75,000 with a further £50,000 outlaid on Raith Rovers front man Keith Wright (21), and with the pair featuring in a three-pronged strike-force alongside the in-form Harvey, Scott's boldness paid off with a 6-3 rout of St Mirren in the next game at Dens Park.

"Tommy Coyne was without doubt the best signing I ever made and Keith Wright wasn't far behind," said Scott. "I'd always admired Coyne and was surprised he hadn't featured more regularly at Tannadice. I'd also been impressed with Wright any time I saw him play - a view reinforced by Stirling Albion and soon to be St Mirren boss Alex Smith, who told me he'd always found Wright a difficult opponent for his side to cope with. So he came highly recommended!"

"Both were proven scorers but were unselfish and would form a potent partnership. Wright was a powerful runner, very direct with a great left-foot shot. Coyne was a really clever player, razor sharp with great movement and just lethal around the box. He was the perfect foil to the more physical Wright who was very strong in the air."

The arrival of these free-scoring strikers came as a tremendous boost and there was a significant improvement in results before the curtain came down on the '86/87 campaign with a 7-3 demolition of already-relegated Hamilton at Dens. "The big disappointment, of course, was our failure to reach the Scottish Cup Final where we would have taken on St Mirren - a game I would have backed us to win," mused Scott. "We lost the semi-final 3-2 to Dundee United at Tynecastle, despite, I believe, being the better side in a real roller-coaster of a game."

"We had lost only one of the four league games against them and were confident of reaching the final but, sadly, two late wonder saves by Billy Thomson prevented us taking it to extra-time which I think we would have won. Nevertheless, we finished on a high and I was relatively happy that my first season in charge meant us maintaining our top-six status of the previous two years under Archie."

That scintillating form continued into season 1987-88 and after the opening five league games, Dundee lay third in the Premier League just a point behind leaders Celtic. Good progress had also been made in the Skol League Cup where victories over Queen's Park and Meadowbank had set the Dark Blues up for a quarter-final derby clash with Dundee United at Dens in early September. "We were playing some brilliant football and with Coyne and Wright bang in form, we had an early chance to make it up to our fans for the Scottish Cup disappointment a few months earlier."

A crowd approaching 20,000 - the biggest at Dens for a number of years - saw the visitors take an early lead through Iain Ferguson, whose two goals had done so much to wreck their hopes at Tynecastle. This time, though, the Coyne-Wright partnership would come out on top and with just five minutes left of a pulsating contest, Dundee's efforts were rewarded when Tommy Coyne knocked home a Tosh McKinlay cross to level the scores.

Dens Park erupted and as Dundee intensified their efforts a brilliant exchange of passes by Harvey and Coyne allowed Keith Wright through to blast home the winner early in extra-time. "I thought the fans were brilliant. The atmosphere and support was unbelievable and it was definitely the best I had experienced at Dens since my playing days," recalled Jocky Scott. Defeating United was always special but winning that particular cup-tie was just terrific and holds a very special memory for me."

"We overcame the psychological barrier of losing that Scottish Cup semi-final as well as the folklore of them winning trophies at Dens Park. I'd told my players that that was history and irrelevant to the latest cup-tie, that the teams were different and everything, including, hopefully, the result, would be too - and it was!" The teams had lined up: *Dundee - Geddes; Glennie, Smith, Duffy; Forsyth, Shannon, Mennie, Angus, McKinlay; Coyne, Wright. Subs. - Harvey, Jack. Dundee United - Thomson; Holt, Hegarty, Narey, Malpas; Bannon, McPhee, Redford, Sturrock; Ferguson, Gallacher. Subs. - Bowman, Irvine.*

The Dens Park boss had played his hand well, starting 3-5-2 before going to 4-3-3 with his late introduction of Harvey from the substitute's bench posing United problems at a crucial time. This was altered again, Scott's decision to deploy a sweeper behind a back four soon after going 2-1 up effectively slamming the door on United's chances of a comeback. "Unfortunately, Jim Duffy suffered extensive cruciate ligament damage at Ibrox soon afterwards which looked to have finished his career, though he made a comeback a couple of years later. It was devastating as he'd been a truly inspirational signing and absolutely outstanding in that cup-tie. I'm quite convinced that if it hadn't happened, we would have beaten Aberdeen in the League Cup semi-final instead of losing two-nil. Sometimes football is all about momentum and of course that hit us really badly and we took a bit of time to get over it."

"We paid £70,000 to bring in Gordon Chisholm from Hibs and he did well but although we won the televised *Tennents Sixes* indoor tournament, it ended up a frustrating season. From a period when anything appeared possible, everything seemed to conspire against us. We had another good win over Dundee United by three goals to one at Tannadice, as well as headline-catching victories over Falkirk (6-0), and Morton (7-1). Tommy Coyne and Keith Wright really were a devastating partnership up front and by early 1988, we looked certainties for a European place and a decent bet for the Scottish Cup."

"However, the board - Angus Cook had recently acquired the major shareholding and taken over as chairman - saw fit to sell John Brown to Rangers for £350,000 in January 1988. Brown, like Duffy, had been a key man, netting 33 goals from midfield in his three and half seasons at Dens and his departure, allied to a series of injuries amongst our most experienced players left us seriously weakened. We'd had an opportunity for the club to kick on but instead ended up seventh and lost out to United in the quarter-finals of the Scottish Cup - a marathon tie which took three games to decide. It was really disappointing."

A year and a half earlier, Scott had done well to revitalise the club by sign-ing Coyne and Wright. At that point, a window of opportunity had existed to encourage a broader-based board of directors and with it the investment that might have taken the club forward. Sadly, that chance was missed and within two years a debt-laden and investment-starved Dundee Football Club would again find themselves relegated to the First Division.

Chapter 10

Dons Red Army

The much-heralded arrival of local businessman Angus Cook, his subsequent acquisition of Dundee FC and elevation to chairman had not brought the anticipated investment and instead rumours that club debts were approaching £500,000 were rife. This, of course, was worrying for Jocky Scott, who still believed that with the right boardroom backing, he could put Dundee back on track, and with just a year left of his current contract, he requested a two-year extension.

To Scott's disappointment, this was refused but, some 66 miles up the road, change was also in the air at Pittodrie where manager Ian Porterfield's two-year reign had come to an end. And when Dons chairman Dick Donald called to propose a new three-man management team of Alex Smith - the ex-St Mirren boss was already a coach at Aberdeen - and Scott as co-managers with Drew Jarvie as their assistant, Scott wasted little time in heading up the A92 to hear more details.

"Some weeks earlier, Drew and I had been out for a post-match drink with our wives in Broughty Ferry. We came across the chairman there and enjoyed a pleasant evening in his company and everything seemed fine. But when my request for a contract extension was later turned down we wondered if he had somebody else in mind, and let it be known to Aberdeen that we would be interested in moving."

"When I told Mr Cook I was resigning, he didn't seem upset. In a way I'd hoped he might have tried to persuade me otherwise but there was nothing in his body language that indicated he wanted me to stay. But in any case it confirmed that Drew and I were right to move on to Aberdeen. However, another director, the former owner, Ian Gellatly advised Angus not to accept my resignation as that might affect any compensation and I understand the club negotiated a £25,000 release deal with Aberdeen. On our departure, Dave Smith, a Dundonian and well acquainted with Mr Cook was appointed as my replacement."

Scott's time as a Dons player had coincided in an upturn in their fortunes and, since then, Aberdeen had gone from strength to strength. Ally McLeod and Billy McNeill had laid the foundations but following McNeill's return to Celtic in 1978, it was the arrival of Alex Ferguson that heralded the finest era in the Pittodrie club's history. Since 1980, Ferguson had masterminded the Dons to European Cup-Winners' Cup glory in Gothenburg, successfully contesting the UEFA Super Cup and lifting no fewer than three Scottish Premier League titles, winning the Scottish Cup four times and the Scottish League Cup on one occasion.

That was an incredible achievement for a provincial club and one which made Ferguson a near impossible act to follow when he left for Manchester United along with Archie Knox in December 1986. Ian Porterfield took over but with little recent knowledge of the Scottish game, he failed to fulfil the sky-high expectations of the fans and with a dearth of silverware and two fourth-place finishes in the league, he and his assistant Jimmy Mullen resigned.

Like the concept of the player-manager, many fans and pundits were dubious about the idea of co-managers. Jocky Scott, though, was more amenable to the new set-up: "Working with Alex Smith, who had led St Mirren to their Scottish Cup success in 1987, was not a problem as we were already good friends after meeting at an SFA coaching course at Largs. We discussed our individual roles at length so there would be no clash of responsibilities and it was agreed that Alex would have the final say on the team. He would also deal with the press and have control of contracts and transfers, while my role was to work with the players out on the training pitch. It suited us both and worked very well."

"When Alex Smith, Drew and I took over, we were fortunate to inherit a very talented squad," said Scott. "Only Willie Miller, Alex McLeish, Neil Simpson and John Hewitt remained from Gothenburg and they formed the core of the team along with another home-grown youngster, David Robertson, who had established himself at left-back. Other stars like Gordon Strachan, Mark McGhee and Eric Black had moved on but the board had invested wisely, bringing in influential ex-Rangers midfielder Jim Bett and the charismatic former Celtic and Arsenal striker Charlie Nicholas. They also signed Robert Connor and Stewart McKimmie, both excellent players who were well known to me from their time at Dundee. And we also had other great competitors like Brian Irvine and Brian Grant with Davie Dodds lending plenty of experience up front."

That summer, Aberdeen had lost Scottish international goalkeeper Jim Leighton, Welsh international midfielder Peter Nicholas and Willie Falconer, who was equally effective as a defender or in his more accustomed role as a striker. "There was concern over how we might replace them but Alex made some excellent signings," said Scott. "Alex Ferguson tipped him off about a contact in Holland and through him we brought in Theo Snelders, Willem van der Ark and Paul Mason for little over £500,000."

"Theo was a big, strapping keeper who instilled great confidence in our defence. Later he was named the Scottish PFA Player of the Year, yet at £270,000 he cost just more than half what we got from Manchester United for Jim Leighton! At 6'5", Van der Ark, with a similar physique to England international Peter Crouch, gave us something different up front while Mason, a Liverpudlian who had worked on a Dutch building site before coming good at Groningen, proved worth his weight in goals from midfield."

In that first season under the new management set-up, a much-improved Aberdeen finished Premier League runners-up to Rangers, who also defeated them 3-2 in a thrilling League Cup Final. That was a re-run of the 1987 final, a footballing classic which ended 3-3 after extra-time with Aberdeen losing out on penalties. Now, Smith and Scott's side had again run the Ibrox side close, a Davie Dodds double leaving the sides tied only for the predatory Ally McCoist to fire home the winner just two minutes from full-time.

There was a recent history of fierce rivalry between the two sets of supporters. In part this was due to the Pittodrie side's dominance throughout the Ferguson era but the situation had been much inflamed after a Neil Simpson tackle resulted in a career-threatening knee injury to talented Ibrox midfielder Ian Durrant two weeks before the '88 League Cup Final. "No-one could deny it was a bad challenge or that Simpson ought to have got a red card rather than the yellow he was shown," said Scott.

"Understandably, Rangers fans felt bitter about the matter but in saying that, the continual dredging up of the topic by certain parts of the media brought an equally hostile reaction from Aberdeen fans and there was regrettable behaviour by both groups of supporters. Even now, almost quarter of a century on, that ill-feeling lingers although not within the clubs themselves."

The Light Blues, with ex-Liverpool and Scotland captain Graeme Souness in charge, were the team to beat for, since 1986, they had invested heavily in the cream of British football, signing a host of top internationalists like Terry Butcher, Chris Woods, Graham Roberts, Ray Wilkins, Richard Gough and Maurice Johnston. This had been facilitated by UEFA's 5-year ban on English clubs competing in Europe following the 1985 Heysel disaster when 39 Italian fans died before the start of the Liverpool v Juventus European Cup Final.

The UEFA ruling meant Rangers could offer the lure of European competition as well as big wages and with that calibre of player, it became all the harder for their domestic competitors. But, having lost to Rangers in 1987 and 1988, it proved third time lucky for the Dons in their third successive League Cup Final against the big-spending Ibrox club on Sunday, October 22nd, 1989.

The Hampden attendance of 61,190 was some 10,000 down on that of the two previous finals, perhaps a reflection on the installation of Rangers as overwhelming favourites. From the team that had ousted Celtic in the semi-final, Ian Cameron - scorer of the only goal - was out with concussion and he and another Alex Smith signing, Craig Robertson made way for up-and-coming 18-year-old striker Eoin Jess and Brian Grant as Aberdeen lined up: *Snelders; McKimmie, McLeish, Miller, Robertson D; Grant, Mason, Bett, Connor; Jess, Nicholas. Subs. - Irvine, Van der Ark. Rangers - Woods; Stevens G, Butcher,*

Gough, Munro; Steven T, Ferguson I, Wilkins, Walters; McCoist, Johnston. Subs. - McCall, Brown.

The Dons got off to a great start when Paul Mason was well-placed to send a fine looping header over the head of England international goalkeeper Chris Woods and into the net. But in 34 minutes, Aberdeen were stunned when Edinburgh referee George Smith awarded a highly contentious penalty, Ally McCoist going down after himself backing into Willie Miller. Walters levelled from the spot but the Dons stood firm and as play ebbed and flowed, there was no separating the sides as the game moved into extra-time. And with 92 minutes on the clock, Paul Mason made it 2-1, drilling the ball home from a clever Charlie Nicholas lay off after a characteristically long throw-in from David Robertson.

Then ensued wave after wave of Rangers attacks but dogged defending and a welcome slice of luck saw Aberdeen hold on to win and the League Cup - or Skol Cup as it had been since 1984 - was Pittodrie bound. That ended a three-year trophy famine and, at a stroke, lifted the pressure from the management team. In next day's *Aberdeen Evening Express* the headlines read *"Cup Full of Cheers"*, *"Sports Express salutes Aberdeen's Skol Cup Superstars"*, and *"Red Heroes Top Character Test"*. The article went on to praise Theo Snelders for his dominating display particularly in extra-time but reserved the top accolade for Jim Bett who was described as: "simply magnificent as he covered every inch of the turf with a first-class display of skill and commitment".

Jocky Scott appeared to have something of a love affair with this particular competition for, having already tasted victory as a player at Dundee in 1973 and Aberdeen three years later, this latest triumph gave him a hat-trick of League Cup winner's medals: "It was a fantastic feeling as a year earlier we'd played really well, taken them all the way - as Aberdeen had done in 1987 - and got nothing. So it was great to return and lift the cup, particularly as we'd beaten both Old Firm clubs in Glasgow to do so," said Scott as he recalled the joy of their Sunday night celebrations at the Marcliffe Hotel in Aberdeen's Queen's Road.

In his post-match conference, Scott and assistant-manger Drew Jarvie were the subject of great praise by Alex Smith: "This is their first success at managerial level and the ideal reward for all their hard work. They are doing a splendid job and I'm confident that more success will follow." Smith's confidence would soon be vindicated for, buoyed by their Skol Cup triumph, Aberdeen returned to the transfer market to splash out a Pittodrie record fee of £650,000 for PSV Eindhoven striker Hans Gillhaus.

"Gillhaus was an inspirational signing and his partnership with Charlie Nicholas was every bit as exciting and effective as the likes of Tommy Coyne and Keith Wright at Dundee, John Robertson and Gary Mackay at Hearts and Ally McCoist and Mo Johnston or Mark Hateley at Rangers," said Scott. "He was good in the air, had a great turn of pace and the ability to run with the ball at defenders but above all he had a brilliant football brain. So, it was money well spent, especially as we got an instant dividend when he netted a double, including a spectacular overhead kick, within the first 11 minutes of his debut, as Aberdeen recorded a 3-0 win against Dunfermline at East End Park."

"And although we didn't really have the depth of squad to trouble Rangers too much in the league that season we were well equipped for the Scottish Cup. We demolished Partick Thistle 6-2 in Glasgow then beat Morton (2-1), and Hearts (4-1), at Pittodrie and a bit like with Dundee in 1974, I felt our name was on the Scottish Cup! In the early '80s, Aberdeen and Dundee United were known as the "New Firm" such was their impact on the Scottish game but although our games with Jim McLean's team were notoriously tight, we dished out a four-nil hammering in the semi-final at Tynecastle - and that was us back at Hampden once again."

Only Celtic stood in the way of a Dons cup double and a 20,000-plus contingent of the "Red Army" were amongst the 60,493 crowd for the Scottish Cup Final on Saturday, May 12th, 1990. Aberdeen showed two changes from their Skol Cup winning side, Gillhaus replacing Jess with Brian Irvine - a scorer in the two previous rounds - preferred to Willie Miller who was only recently back after a bad knee injury. *Aberdeen - Snelders; McKimmie, McLeish, Irvine, Robertson; Mason, Grant, Bett, Connor; Nicholas, Gillhaus. Subs. - Jess, Watson. Celtic - Bonner; Wdowczyk, Elliot, Whyte, Rogan; Stark, McStay, Grant; Miller, Walker, Dziekanowski. Subs. - Coyne, Galloway.*

Celtic were a shadow of the side that had won the title in their Centenary season of 1987-88, thereafter finishing third and now fifth in the league. And despite the undoubted quality of strikers like "Jackie" Dziekanowski, Tommy Coyne and Andy Walker, they had managed only 37 league goals, 19 less than the Dons, who were strong favourites to win. Early on, Nicholas was thwarted by a Paul Elliot goal-line clearance but with Gillhaus well marshalled by the Parkhead defender, the battling Celts took Aberdeen all the way. A no-scoring stalemate was followed by a tension-ridden half-hour of extra-time then for the first time, a Scottish Cup Final was decided by penalty shoot-out.

Alex McLeish won the toss and the right to have the kicks taken at the "Rangers" end in front of the massed Aberdeen support. But with Celtic's Dariusz Wdowczyk and the Dons' Brian Grant of the five designated kickers failing to score, it was on to sudden death. The quality of the spot-kicks was superb but with the score 8-8 on penalties, Snelders remained static until the last moment and managed to push aside Anton Rogan's effort.

Aberdeen Evening Express columnist Bill McKenzie described the conclusion to the drama: "Now Brian Irvine was faced with the equally daunting task of outwitting Pat Bonner to win the cup. If the quiet man of Pittodrie was enduring a living hell, he didn't show it as he coolly sent Bonner one way and the ball into the opposite corner. It was over, the cup was on its way back north and the elation of the players as they embraced Irvine and Snelders told its own story!"

Later Alex Smith confessed: "I'd feel sorry for any team that loses on penalties but that's the rule now and we are just delighted to have won the cup." Jocky Scott agreed saying: "It felt great, just great - my first Scottish Cup Final and it's a winner. Maybe we didn't play as well as we can but we won the cup and that's the main thing. We knew that Jim Bett's midfield battle with Paul McStay would be crucial and with Jim coming out on top in that particular battle, I always felt we had a slight edge."

"We stopped overnight at Anstruther in Fife for a celebration dinner and drinks and returned to Aberdeen on the Sunday. At the Bridge of Dee we switched to an open top bus and travelled along Great Southern Road, up Holburn Street and along Union Street before coming to a halt outside the Town House, where a joyous mass of fans gathered to cheer the players and officials. It really was a great day. And of course for a provincial club that had somewhat slipped out of the limelight, to have completed a cup double as well as finishing second for the second successive season made it a helluva season for Aberdeen!"

The Smith-Scott management team then had proved highly successful and Scott's coaching was held in the highest regard at Pittodrie, where the players greatly respected his footballing knowledge and training methods. For his part, Jocky Scott loved every minute of his time on the training ground: "We concentrated a lot on organisation but always encouraged the players to express themselves. The experienced guys set a good example and the Dutch contingent were different class and really professional in their preparation for games. It was a great experience for me working with such high quality players and very satisfying to see youngsters like Eoin Jess, Scott Booth and Stephen Wright coming through the ranks to establish themselves in the first-team."

"It really was an incredible period," recalled Scott. "Aberdeen had the cash as well as a great footballing reputation in those days. They could afford to spend well over half a million pounds for a striker like Gillhaus - who had won a European Cup winner's medal for PSV against Benfica - also outlaying a similar amount to bring in Snelders, Van der Ark and Mason. Yet compared to the Fergie era, that team tends to be under-rated though, arguably, we had the best footballing side in Scotland at the time. Indeed, five of our players - Alex McLeish, Stewart McKimmie and Jim Bett for Scotland, and Theo Snelders and Hans Gillhaus for Holland - were included in their country's World Cup squads for the finals at Italia '90."

The league championship was the one prize to have eluded Jocky Scott so it was fitting that Aberdeen were finally to make a late run to challenge strong-going Rangers for the 1990-91 Scottish Premier League title. The return of Charlie Nicholas on freedom of contract to Celtic had been a blow and despite the arrival of Dutch holding midfielder Peter Van de Ven, it was, somewhat perversely, a first-round Scottish Cup defeat by eventual winners Motherwell which was to kick-start an Aberdeen revival.

The Dons had trailed Rangers by seven points with 10 games to go, but manager Graeme Souness's surprise departure for Liverpool in April saw the Light Blues stumble and, almost incredibly, a fine run of form put Aberdeen back in contention. On the penultimate day of the season, Rangers crashed 3-0 at Motherwell and with goals by Van der Ark and young Scott Booth earning a 2-1 win over St Johnstone at Pittodrie, the Dons went top of the table on goal-difference. Having won 11 of their previous 12 games (the other was drawn), the momentum was very much with them. And now, just a single point against Rangers at Ibrox would see them lift the title for the first time since 1985.

The scene was set for a dramatic last day finale although Theo Snelders would be missing. The inspirational keeper had recovered from a fractured cheekbone sustained against Rangers in October only to recently suffer a dislocated shoulder against Hibs and 20-year-old Michael Watt would continue in goals. From the previous game, Jess returned for Booth, while Van der Ark - recently a regular alongside Jess and Gillhaus - made way for Van de Ven as Aberdeen fielded - *Watt; Wright, McLeish, McKimmie, Robertson D; Grant, Bett, Van de Ven, Connor; Jess, Gillhaus. Subs. - Van der Ark, Booth. Rangers - Woods; Stevens, Nisbet, Spackman, Cowan; Walters, Ferguson, Hurlock, Brown; Hateley, Johnston. Subs. - Durrant, McCoist.*

With less than a minute played, Michael Watt looked set to collect a long, high ball into his penalty box only to be sent crashing by Mark Hateley. The young keeper required extensive treatment before being able to continue but no free-kick was awarded by referee Brian McGinlay. That incident set the tone and with the tackling intense, an incredible 48 fouls were recorded as play raged from end to end. Bett, Van de Ven and Gillhaus all had chances as Aberdeen gave as good as they got but in 40 minutes Hateley outjumped McLeish to head the opener. And when the big Rangers striker added a second after Watt spilled a Johnston shot soon after half-time, it was all over for the Dons despite Van der Ark then substituting for Van de Ven.

In an interview with *Heraldsport* 20 years later, Scott Booth recalled that Aberdeen had had to change in a Portakabin due to work in one of the dressing rooms and that their fans had been allocated just 3,000 tickets within Ibrox stadium which then had a capacity of just over 37,000. "It was the most hostile environment I ever played in. I remember coming on at half-time and finding it hard to concentrate. It was absolutely deafening. Guys like myself and Michael Watt, I think it's quite natural if we were slightly overawed by it all."

"I don't know who decided what, but the general consensus was that there had been a change in tactics. We had been playing 4-3-3, a very carefree system, but at Ibrox we went to 4-4-2. Maybe that change from something that was working disrupted us, I don't know. It's easy to say in hindsight they got it wrong though we actually started the better side."

As senior manager, Alex Smith was the man with the ultimate decision but, for his part, Jocky Scott said: "Regardless of what system was used we had enough chances to win but didn't take them. But by changing what was a successful formula we laid ourselves open to criticism. Each Wednesday, Alex, Drew and I sat down to discuss the forthcoming game. We knew Rangers would have had us watched and, hoping to surprise them, decided to tweak the system to 4-4-2. Initially, I think it worked as we had some great chances before they went ahead but Hateley deliberately barged into young Michael Watt and got away with it. He should have been sent off."

Following their defeat at Fir Park, Rangers had to go all-out for victory whereas Aberdeen had the option of trying to settle for a point. Geed up by Walter Smith and his newly appointed assistant Archie Knox - equally well known by Dons fans for his time at Pittodrie and Jocky Scott for his time at Dens – tough-tackling Rangers were determined not to allow Aberdeen to settle to their usual pattern. Consequently, Aberdeen struggled to get their more cultured game going and were hardly helped by the leniency shown by referee McGinlay towards a succession of fouls committed not just by Hateley, but also by others, particularly the fiercely combatative midfielder Terry Hurlock, whose crude challenge ensured the withdrawal of Jess at half-time.

In the big-match post-mortem, the *Aberdeen Evening Express* remarked how: "The whole league campaign had come down to 90 jangling minutes and on the day the side which coped best with the pressure of the occasion emerged victorious. There could be no complaints from the understandably downhearted Dons." In the following Saturday's *Green Final* Postbag, many readers were critical of the decision to switch from 4-3-3, some lamenting that there was not an experienced goalkeeper in reserve, while others believed Brian Irvine should have been brought back to combat Hateley's physical presence. Most though were full of praise for Aberdeen's league challenge, which they said had provided them with some of the most entertaining football for years.

However, the hangover of losing out on the big prize - exacerbated by the sale of David Robertson to Rangers for £970,000 - spilled over into the '91/92 campaign. And when Aberdeen, having previously exited the League

Cup to Airdrie, lost their first round, first-leg UEFA Cup tie to BK 1903 Copenhagen one-nil, around 300 supporters demonstrated noisily behind the main stand at Pittodrie. They were looking for change but so too was Jocky Scott, who now believed it was time for him to again assume greater responsibility, preferably at Aberdeen. He communicated his feelings to Alex Smith but Smith, although not against an eventual move "upstairs", felt it was too early to relinquish full managerial control.

Dunfermline Athletic had just sacked Iain Munro and in late September, Scott received a call from chairman Roy Woodrow offering him the chance to become manager at East End Park: "It was a difficult decision for me. Dunfermline were toiling and it was likely to be a struggle to keep them up. On the other hand it was an opportunity to have full control again, so after considerable deliberation and discussion with my wife, I decided to accept. It was a wrench leaving a club like Aberdeen where I had many happy memories as a player as well as a coach. I particularly remember with some fondness former chairman Dick Donald who was himself a former player with the Dons."

Donald indeed had played for the Dons for 10 years interrupted only for a season with Dunfermline Athletic before retiring from the game in 1939. He returned a decade later to join the board, became vice chairman in 1960 and chairman 10 years later. "Dick Donald would always come in to the dressing room before every match to wish the boys good luck and regardless of the result always popped in after the game as well. He was by far the best chairman that I ever had."

All that though was in the past and a new chapter in Scott's career was about to unfold.

Chapter 11

East Ender

In the 1960s, Dunfermline Athletic were one of Scotland's top provincial sides. Back then, when coal was king in the Kingdom of Fife, the men in black and white stripes were a team to be reckoned with. They had won the Scottish Cup in 1961 and 1968, were beaten finalists in 1965 and had also reached the semi-finals in the two previous years. Many a great European night was seen at East End Park with famous victories over the likes of Everton and Valencia before the Pars reached the European Cup-Winners' Cup semi-final in 1969.

The great Jock Stein was manager for the early part of that era and there were heroes aplenty such as goalkeeper Eddie Connachan, wingers Alex Edwards, George Peebles and Harry Melrose, and goal-scorers like Charlie Dickson and Alex Ferguson - the latter going on to fame and fortune as manager of Aberdeen and Manchester United.

These days, however, were long gone. Like other prominent provincial clubs, the introduction of the new 10-team Premier League in 1975 made it tough for the Fifers to maintain their position amongst the elite of Scottish football. Dunfermline found themselves out of the top tier, even dropping to the Second Division. And although they bounced back, most recently in 1989, they again found it hard going and for the past two years had flirted dangerously with the drop.

By the time of Jocky Scott's arrival, they lay rooted to the foot of the Premier League but in marked contrast to their league form, a series of favourable results against Alloa, St Mirren and Dundee United had brought them within 90 minutes of an appearance in the Scottish League Cup Final. That, of course was a competition in which Scott had excelled, having already secured winner's medals as a player for Dundee and Aberdeen, and another as co-manager of the Dons alongside Alex Smith.

Now, in just his second game in charge, Dunfermline faced Airdrie in the semi-final at Tynecastle. And although the recently promoted Diamonds were one of Scotland's less fashionable clubs, the wily Scott was under no illusions: "I hadn't been there that long but in an earlier round while still at Pittodrie, Airdrie had beaten Aberdeen then gone on to eliminate Celtic on penalties. So, I knew that we were in for an extremely tough game!"

It was all of that and certainly no game for the purist as Alex MacDonald's fiercely competitive Broomfield outfit contested every ball. But the battling Pars gave as good as they got and despite trailing to an Owen Coyle goal, they were rewarded when Derek McWilliams netted a late leveller from the

72

spot. With the score tied 1-1 after extra-time, it was on to a penalty shoot-out and in a dramatic finale, Dunfermline triumphed by three goals to two with skipper Norrie McCathie stepping up to fire home the winning goal and spark wild scenes of celebration!

The Fifers could now look forward to their first cup final in 23 years but league form had been poor and strong-going Hibernian, conquerors of Rangers in the other semi-final, were firm favourites to win. A crowd of 40,377 turned out for the Skol-sponsored League Cup Final on October 27th, 1991 as the teams lined up: *Dunfermline - Rhodes; Wilson, McCathie, Moyes, Sharp; Robertson, Kozma, Davies, McWilliams; Leitch, Sinclair. Subs. - McCall, Cunnington. Hibernian - Burridge; Miller, Hunter, McIntyre, Mitchell; Weir, Hamilton, McLeod, McGinlay; Wright, Evans. Subs. - Orr, Beaumont.*

Scott made four changes from the semi-final, introducing Tommy Wilson, Istvan Kozma, Chris Sinclair and Billy Davies for Eddie Cunnington, Mark Haro, Ian McParland and Ian McCall. Dunfermline held their own and with the half-time score-line blank, Hibs looked increasingly edgy until Tommy McIntyre put them ahead with a 49th-minute penalty. Thereafter, it was an uphill struggle and with just four minutes remaining, Scott's former Dens Park prodigy Keith Wright slipped home a second to seal the Fifers' fate.

Earlier that month, Jocky Scott had appointed his friend and former team-mate Gordon Wallace as his assistant with Dundee later understood to have received compensation after Wallace's resignation as Dens boss. Afternoon training sessions were introduced with the players lunching together at East End Park beforehand to bolster team spirit. However, there was also an urgent need for reinforcements and with the backing of the board, four experienced players were brought in.

Dundee's Scotland Under-21 international defender Rab Shannon arrived in exchange for Pars midfield playmaker Ian McCall and Eddie Gallagher plus cash; in too came the competitive former Aberdeen, Aston Villa and Rangers midfielder Neal Cooper along with ex-Dundee United fringe striker John Reilly. But the pick of the newcomers was another Tannadice player, the former Highland League Keith front man Hamish French, who was obtained for a six figure fee.

"Reilly never really kicked a ball for us through injury but Cooper and Shannon, who was versatile, did us a turn and French was a class act up front." There was an improvement but despite a run of just one defeat in seven league games, the sale of Hungarian international midfielder Istvan Kozma to Liverpool for £300,000 in February meant the writing was on the wall for Dunfermline. "Kozma was a skilful, creative player, a real fans' favourite who'd been signed for a record £540,000 a few years earlier. The directors felt it was an offer they could not refuse, but his departure came at a bad time for us and we ended bottom of the Premier League, said Scott."

"Moving to Dunfermline was one of my biggest regrets and it was a mistake for me to leave Pittodrie where we'd won the Scottish and League Cups and also finished league runners-up three seasons running. Aberdeen and Dundee were big city clubs, whereas the town of Dunfermline had a population of around 50,000. I didn't enjoy my last experience of fighting relegation back in '83/84 in Archie Knox's first season at Dens Park but, thereafter, Dundee and Aberdeen were both on the up in my time there. And once you're used to challenging at the top end of the table, it's hard going struggling at the bottom."

"As well as the guys I signed, we had a nucleus of pretty decent players like Andy Rhodes in goal, central defenders Norrie McCathie and Davie Moyes, Craig Robertson, Billy Davies and the hard-working Derek McWilliams in midfield and Scott Leitch up front. However, we finished six points behind St Mirren - who also went down - and sixteen behind third-bottom Motherwell. We managed just four league wins, scoring only 22 goals and conceding 80, which was abysmal. It really was a dreadful season and there's no getting away from the fact we lacked quality throughout the side," admitted Scott. "However, we drew around a third of our fixtures and if some of those had been turned into wins, we might have given ourselves a chance of staying up."

"The Scottish League set-up then was 12-12-14 with two clubs promoted from the First Division. Ourselves and the Paisley Saints were favourites to go back up but I was wary of Killie and Hamilton and thought Raith Rovers capable of better things. Our average home gate in the Premier League had been around 6,400, so First Division football and greatly reduced attendances meant the club taking a big financial hit. Effectively, Dunfermline needed to get straight back up and that put myself and Gordon Wallace under considerable pressure. We exchanged Andy Rhodes for St Johnstone keeper Lindsay Hamilton and their striker Roddy Grant and made a pretty good start to the campaign. Only two of our initial 11 games were lost but the second quarter was a nightmare with three times as many defeats."

Dunfermline had quickly found themselves facing an uphill struggle to keep pace with their big Fife rivals, Raith Rovers. Jimmy Nicholl, the former Manchester United, Rangers and Northern Ireland international defender, had spent a season at Dunfermline before becoming player-manager at Raith in 1990. There he had installed a winning mentality, building an attractive team around himself and others like Shaun Dennis, Gordon Dalziel, Colin Cameron and Stevie Crawford and now the Kirkcaldy side had set a cracking pace at the top.

"Until then, I'd only experienced the Dundee derby but derbies are just as keenly contested between, obviously the Old Firm and Hibs and Hearts, but also Killie and Ayr, St Mirren and Morton or as I then discovered,

Dunfermline and Raith Rovers. Kirkcaldy is 14 miles from Dunfermline but the rivalry is intense and with the added edge of both clubs pushing for promotion, I think three of our derby clashes attracted gates of around 6,000 with a bumper 10,600 crowd turning out for the East End Park clash at New Year."

"Raith were a very good side and when we lost to them for a third time in late March, it virtually confirmed them as champions. However, Dunfermline had won nine and drawn two of their games in the third quarter and with five of our remaining eight matches at home we were confident of going up. It looked a straight fight between ourselves and Kilmarnock for the second promotion place so a 2-2 draw with them at home at least meant we hadn't lost any ground," said Scott.

However, a shock home reverse to Stirling Albion then the loss of a point at Clydebank set the alarm bells ringing, and the slump continued with a 2-1 defeat to St Mirren at East End Park. The goals had dried up at the worst possible time with Roddy Grant, who'd scored plenty of goals at Perth, failing to live up to expectations. However, a Hamish French goal for the third successive game brought a 1-0 win at Meadowbank giving Dunfermline a two-point lead over Kilmarnock, and with just three games remaining - against Cowdenbeath (h), Dumbarton (a), and Morton (h) - the finishing line was in sight.

Alas, the nightmare of seeing Raith Rovers achieve championship glory was now exacerbated by a crushing two-nil defeat to another Fife side, bottom-of-the-league Cowdenbeath. As Dunfermline crumbled, the "Blue Brazil" had raised their game and with Killie taking both points to move ahead on goal-difference, manager Scott and his players were mercilessly booed at the full-time whistle.

Another faltering performance in a 0-0 draw at Dumbarton coupled with a Killie win at Cowdenbeath left matters out of Dunfermline's hands. Now a point behind, only a victory over Morton and a Hamilton win at Rugby Park would suffice but any prospect of a last day redemption ended with the Pars losing 2-1 and the Ayrshire side celebrating promotion after a goalless draw. "Words cannot describe how I felt in those final few weeks. It just slipped away from us. The Morton game was typical in that we made countless chances, didn't take them then found ourselves two down. We didn't get any breaks but you need to make things happen to earn that bit of luck and too often we didn't do that," said Scott.

Damningly, the Pars, who had lost their last four home fixtures, had won only one of their final nine games, and early the following week Jocky Scott and Gordon Wallace were sacked. "It was expected and I had no gripe with the decision," said Scott. We were tasked with keeping the club in the Premier League, then the target was to get them back up but we didn't do that either. After what we'd had at Aberdeen, I found it hard to accept that there were not enough winners in the Dunfermline squad. However, you could never level that accusation at David Moyes, Billy Davies or even Ian McCall in the short time I had him there."

"These guys in particular always gave their all - at training or in matches - and they took that attitude with them when they went into management. They all did well, Moyes at Preston and Everton before joining Manchester United, Davies at Motherwell, Preston, Derby and at Nottingham Forest (twice); and McCall at Clydebank, Morton, Airdrie, Falkirk, Dundee United, Queen of the South and Partick Thistle. Of course, they had their own ideas about things which they were entitled to, but after I'd left East End Park, I heard it said that they hadn't liked the manner in which I made my demands on players on match days. Well, all I can say is that I would've liked to have been a fly on the wall when their teams were having a bad day!"

"Big Norrie McCathie was another with a great attitude and was Dunfermline through and through. He played well over 500 games and would've run through a brick wall for that club. It was an absolute tragedy when he and a girlfriend died from carbon monoxide poisoning at his home in early 1996. That was the second tragedy to hit the club after Gary Riddell's death during a half-marathon to raise money after the Hillsborough crowd disaster in 1989. So, as you can well imagine, those tragic events put the game of football and my grumbles into their true perspective," concluded Scott.

Scott, nevertheless, had found his failure at Dunfermline a deeply disheartening experience and envisaged a few months break to recharge his batteries before returning to the game. Instead, his sabbatical proved far longer and it was January 1994 before he took over at Second Division Arbroath, replacing former Celtic and Scotland international full-back Danny McGrain, who had resigned due to ill-health.

"That was the first time I'd been sacked and I'd no idea what was involved in agreeing a settlement," admitted Scott. "It was a time-consuming business and all the legal twists and turns made it difficult for me to accept another job without it having an adverse effect on my severance package," he recalled. "However, once the financial arrangements were finally agreed, I was approached by Arbroath committee chairman John Christison and after consideration, accepted the job as manager."

"To be honest, I really had no inclination towards part-time football as I'd been full-time all my life. On the other hand I felt that if I did well it might provide me with a stepping-stone back to full-time football. It's sometimes easier to get another post when you're in employment and in the public eye rather than being out of the game entirely so I decided to accept the position," he said.

Its ancient Abbey apart, the red sandstone town of Arbroath was perhaps best known as a small fishing port and as a holiday destination featuring an outdoor bathing pool, carnival and miniature railway. In contrast, the football club's main claim to fame was their 36-0 victory over Bon Accord in 1885, a long-standing world record in professional football. Most of the club's history had been spent in the lower leagues and only in the late 1930s, season 1959-60, and for four years between 1968 and 1975 - had the "Red Lichties" graced the top level in what was then Scottish League Division One.

Arbroath played at Gayfield Park, a neat, well-maintained ground whose south side is close to the North Sea leaving it vulnerable to the elements in stormy weather. Albert Henderson was one of the longest-serving managers in British football, serving Arbroath from 1962 until 1979. There were prolific post-war scorers like Dave Easson (late '50s), Jimmy Jack and Denis Bruce ('60s), and Billy Pirie and Jimmy Bone ('70s); left-half Tom Cargill made a record 445 appearances, while two of Henderson's ex-Dundee teammates, Andy Penman and Hugh Robertson, brought a dash of flair to the Lichties sides of the early 1970s whilst in the twilight of their careers.

These days were gone, however - the local fishing fleet entering a terminal decline, the Scottish seaside trip largely superseded by the cheaper package holiday abroad and iconic buildings such as the Art Deco style outdoor pool falling into disrepair before being demolished. Similarly, the advent of the smaller Premier League and the new three-league set-up in 1975 was a defining moment for smaller clubs like Arbroath, who thereafter struggled to maintain a promotion challenge against wealthier full-time opponents.

Soon, they mostly found themselves in the lowest tier with home gates, previously averaging 2,000 to 3,500 in the '60s and '70s, seriously affected by the club's downward spiral. Scott's predecessor, a popular figure with Arbroath supporters who rebranded themselves "*Danny McGrain's Bearded Army*" had taken the club to sixth in the 14-team Second Division in '92/93. More recently, though, Arbroath had endured a 9-1 thrashing by Celtic in the League Cup and league form had been erratic before McGrain called it a day due to illness.

The stability of the Henderson era had gone and as Arbroath's ninth manager in almost 14 years, Jocky Scott had no illusions about the difficulty of his task. However, he made a good start with a 2-1 victory over Alloa Athletic at Recreation Park and, despite a four-nil midweek defeat at Berwick, it was like old times as Arbroath played host to Dundee United in the third-round of the Scottish Cup. There was no disgrace as the "Red Lichties" went down 3-2 to the Premier League side before a sell-out 5,961 crowd but soon Scott was having serious misgivings about his new post.

The teams for the Scottish Cup tie at Gayfield on January 29th had been: *Arbroath - Jackson; Farnan, Mitchell, Adam, Florence; Martin, King, McKinnon,*

Clouston; Diver, Sorbie. Subs. - Scott, Buckley. Dundee United - Van de Kamp; Van der Hoorn, Clelland, Petric, Malpas; Bowman, McInally, McKinlay; Crabbe, Brewster, Connolly. Subs. - Dailly, Nixon.

"Monday and Thursday were the training nights but Danny McGrain had signed a good number of west coast players and, rather than travel to Arbroath, allowed them to train with a club near their home. It meant I had only three first-team players training along with the kids and after a few weeks of this I had had enough so demanded every player report to training next Monday night. We worked out on Gayfield under the floodlights and after an excellent session, I told the players that that was to be a regular night for all the first-team," said Scott.

"The guys went for a shower, I went to my office and had just sat down with a coffee when there was a knock on my door. In came a player to inform me he couldn't travel to Arbroath every Monday so felt he had to ask for a transfer. No sooner had he left than another player came in and said the same thing and within 10 minutes all the travellers had come in and asked for a transfer. It was then I realised part-time football was not for me."

"Results weren't great - just one win, five draws and eight defeats from my 14 games there. But it wasn't my team, it would take time to change and in those circumstances I decided to go," sighed Scott. "I approached the chairman and indicated I would continue only as long as it took for the club to acquire a new manager. By mid-April, Donald Park and my former Dens Park team-mate George Mackie had been lined up and just 12 weeks after taking up the reins at Gayfield, I was released from my contract!"

Chapter 12

Hibernian

Networking is an important form of communication whether it be in industry, commercial life or indeed football. In the past three years, Jocky Scott's managerial star had waned and now more than anything, the Aberdonian needed a change in fortune. The SFA coaching school at Largs was a centre of football learning but also a forum for football people to exchange views and it was there that many friendships in the game were forged.

Craig Brown, Alex Smith and Walter Smith were men who Scott knew well but it was his acquaintanceship with another Largs regular, Hibs boss and former Rangers defender Alex Miller that was now to prove useful. So, when Andy Watson left the Easter Road assistant-manager's job to rejoin former Dons team-mate Alex McLeish at Motherwell, Miller, who was an admirer of Scott's coaching abilities, sounded him out and the Aberdonian was more than happy to accept the vacancy.

Elated at his return to full-time football, Scott, along with his wife Elaine and a couple of friends went out to celebrate but what should have been a happy occasion turned into a nightmare when he received news that his father had passed away. "When something like that occurs it puts everything into perspective and to this day I still feel the shock of that call," recalled Jocky. However, I just had to get on with things and, following the frustration of part-time management at Arbroath, I looked forward to getting back to working with players on a daily basis again.

There is no doubt that Hibernian are a club steeped in tradition and one of the biggest names in Scottish football. Hibs, nicknamed the "Hibees", are traditionally identified with a cavalier-type approach to playing the game with their "Famous Five" front line of Gordon Smith, Bobby Johnstone, Lawrie Reilly, Eddie Turnbull and Willie Ormond spearheading them to Scottish League Championship victories in 1948, 1950 and 1951 in what was truly a halcyon post-war era for the Easter Road club.

Hibs had been the first British club to play in the inaugural European Cup in 1955, but despite the emergence of star attackers like Joe Baker, Willie Hamilton, Neil Martin and Colin Stein in the late 50's and '60s, they were able to build little of substance. The great Jock Stein was manager for an all -too-brief spell, leading Hibs to Summer Cup glory in 1964 before returning to Celtic after less than a year. Bob Shankly did well enough but, as at Dundee, too many big names were sold against his wishes and it was the early 1970s with Eddie Turnbull back as manager before Hibs were again a side to be reckoned with.

Those were the days of "Turnbull's Tornadoes" and with great players like Pat Stanton, John Blackley, John Brownlie, Alex Cropley and Arthur Duncan gracing the famous green and white jersey, there was League Cup success against Celtic in 1972 and Drybrough Cup wins in '72 and '73. In 1980, the club were relegated from the Premier League but bounced back only to face a battle for survival against an attempted "merger" with local rivals Hearts led by Wallace Mercer in 1990. However, in response to this threat, supporters successfully initiated the "Hands off Hibs" campaign and with prominent local businessman Tom Farmer at the helm, signings of the calibre of Murdo McLeod and Keith Wright propelled Hibs to another League Cup success in 1991.

Just as he was aware of their history, Jocky Scott recognised the potential at Easter Road: "Hibs are one of Scotland's most famous clubs who play in Edinburgh, the capital. Back then, they had some top quality players like Darren Jackson and Michael O'Neill, who were internationalists with Scotland and Northern Ireland while there were others who were also capable of competing with the best. So the opportunity was there for them to develop into one of the top teams in Scotland."

Victories against Queen of the South and Dunfermline took the Easter Road men to the League Cup quarter-finals but any hopes of glory were quickly dispelled by a shock 2-1 defeat to First Division Airdrie. Nevertheless, the Alex Miller - Jocky Scott combination worked well and by the turn of the year, Hibs lay third in the league. All connected with the club were well aware that it was 1902 when they had last won the Scottish Cup but this time many believed the Leith side had the necessary grit and flair for success, with Jocky Scott certain they could go all the way.

"Defensively we were sound, while up front Keith Wright and Darren Jackson were a great partnership. We had a good balance in midfield and could use lads like Gareth Evans, ex-Falkirk and Chelsea man Kevin McAllister or the fast-emerging Kevin Harper wide right," said Scott. "McAllister was exciting to watch and on his day a match winner. Pat McGinlay, who'd returned after a 14-month spell at Celtic, was a tireless runner, the perfect foil for the hugely talented Michael O'Neill on the left. Michael was more stylish, a flair player with a bit of edge and a regular for Northern Ireland who went on to manage his country. Both, however, could find the net and that season they got 23 goals between them."

In the third round, Hibs won 2-0 at lower league Montrose and a similar score line at Easter Road saw them past strongly-fancied Motherwell for a place in the last eight. The cup draw sent Miller's men to Second Division Stenhousemuir but with the Warriors fresh from a coupon-busting two-nil fourth-round win over Aberdeen which cost Dons boss Willie Miller his job, Miller and Scott had to ensure their team's attitude was correct. The tiny

Ochilview ground was bursting at the seams but although duffle-coated home boss Terry Christie, a self-confessed Hibs fan, had his team well up for the tie, Hibs matched them for commitment and ran out comfortable 4-0 winners.

City rivals Hearts were also through, but any hopes of an all-Edinburgh final collapsed when they fell 1-0 to the "awkward squad" of Airdrie. Hibs, meanwhile, faced Celtic in their semi-final with Jocky Scott reflecting: "We would've preferred to avoid Celtic for despite losing to Airdrie in the League Cup, we felt we could have handled them at Hampden. Even so, we were confident of beating Celtic as we were a couple of points ahead of them in the league. And since we had not conceded any goals in the competition thus far, we believed ourselves well capable of reaching the final in May."

Bizarrely for these times, the Hibs v Celtic semi-final took place on a Friday evening at Ibrox Park on April 7th. The SFA had judged this to be the best neutral venue as Celtic, whose ground was under reconstruction, were playing their home games at Hampden Park that season, Rangers were at home to Aberdeen in the league the following day, and with the Hearts tie at Hampden on the Sunday, the authorities were anxious to avoid any possible clash between the two sets of Edinburgh fans in or travelling to Glasgow.

The Ibrox tie ended in a 0-0 draw and although Hibs had their chances to score, they had a let-off when Jim Leighton saved a 75th-minute Andy Walker penalty after the Celtic striker grabbed the ball from former Hibs midfielder John Collins, their regular penalty-taker. It had been Hibernian's misfortune to be without the injured Kevin McAllister and central-defender and skipper Gordon Hunter, the latter nicknamed "GBH" for his battling spirit and unswerving commitment to the club he had supported as a boy.

And with both still missing from the replay at the same venue four days later the sides lined up: *Hibernian - Leighton; Miller, Tweed, Millen, Mitchell; Harper, McGinlay, McGraw, O'Neill; Jackson, Wright. Subs. Tortolano, Evans. Celtic - Bonner; Boyd, Vata, O'Neil, McKinlay; McStay, McLaughlin, Grant, Collins; Walker, Falconer. Subs. - O'Donnell, Donnelly.*

The attendance of 32,410 was almost 25% down on the first tie but while Mark McGraw had been brought in for the more defensive Davie Farrell, it was the introduction of ex-Don Willie Falconer who replaced the injured Pierre van Hooijdonk that had the bigger impact. He netted Celtic's second goal after Collins put them ahead and although Wright pulled one back midway through the second half, Phil O'Donnell made it 3-1 for the Hoops, who went on to lift the cup - manager Tommy Burns' sole success and their first trophy for six years.

It was an opportunity lost for Hibs, for just a few months earlier Celtic had suffered an ignominious defeat to First Division Raith Rovers in the

Coca Cola Cup Final at Ibrox and confidence was fragile. Nevertheless, Scott and Miller could be proud of what they had done that season. Their third-place Premier League finish was the highest the Easter Road club had managed since 1976 and was ample testimony to their hard work on the training ground. Just as importantly, Hibs had finally ended their 22-game derby drought against city rivals Hearts.

The hoodoo had lasted from April 1989 until a thundering shot by Gordon Hunter brought a 1-0 victory at Tynecastle the previous August. A 2-1 home win followed a couple of months later and in May 1995, there was a 3-1 derby triumph at Easter Road before a much-reduced 7,146 crowd due to the construction of the two new stands behind the goals. "We'd finally cracked the derby bogey, did well in league and cup and our next goal was to go one step better and actually bring silverware to Easter Road," said Scott. We felt we were not that far away from being a really good side and next season couldn't come soon enough!"

"Keith Wright had a real physical presence, got us goals and was a great guy to have in your team. He was very unselfish and I'm sure he'll still tell you that Tommy Coyne (from Dundee) and Darren Jackson - who both went to Celtic - got their moves due to him! He was worth every penny of the £500,000 Hibs paid Dundee for him in 1991 and both he and George Stewart before him were keen Hibees who did really well at Easter Road. Like Coyne, Jackson, who was always on the alert for Wright's lay-offs, was an intelligent player with clever movement. He had a bit of devil about him, made things happen around the box and was a good finisher."

Somehow, though, things did not go as planned and the '95/96 campaign ended with Hibs slipping two places in the league and making a premature exit from both cup competitions Even worse, they ended 12 points behind city rivals Hearts and there were increasing signs of unrest amongst the Easter Road faithful. "For years Hibs had a solid full-back partnership of Willie Miller and Graham Mitchell, but with Mitchell at the veteran stage and Miller out injured, that area was disrupted. Some of the youngsters who came in weren't good enough, while others like Weir - who'd spent a lot of time on the treatment table - and Hunter were maybe past their best," said Scott."

"At the end of that season, we lost two important players. Michael O'Neill was transferred to Coventry City for £660,000 while Scotland-Under-21 international central-defender Steven Tweed joined the Greek club Ionikis on freedom of contract. To replace them, Alex Miller had already brought in Chelsea's Andy Dow, a creative left-sided player for £125,000, with Dundee United centre-half Brian Welsh arriving for £200,000, St Mirren striker Barry Lavety for the same amount with Partick Thistle's ex-Aberdeen midfielder Ian Cameron coming in exchange for the surplus to requirements Davie Farrell and Gareth Evans.

In the '96/97 League Cup, Hibs cruised past Brechin City and Albion Rovers only to find Rangers an insurmountable barrier in the quarter-finals. That 4-0 reverse at Ibrox followed a 5-0 thrashing at Celtic and when Hearts, who had dramatically beaten Celtic and would go on to the final, left Easter Road with a 3-1 victory in late September, it was all over for Alex Miller. In his 10 years in charge, he had consistently achieved an upper mid-table status and had taken Hibs to two League Cup Finals but only rarely had Hibs finished above Hearts in the league. Now, once again, the Tynecastle side were in the ascendancy and, perhaps just as significantly, many fans perceived Miller's cautious style of football foreign to that traditionally associated with the club and the writing was on the wall.

Alex Miller leaving Hibernian had caught Jocky Scott by surprise: "It was a shock. I had no idea that he was leaving. In fact when Alex said to me that he was away, I thought he meant he was off home and replied that I'd see him tomorrow!" For Scott, there were fears that he might follow Miller out the door but instead he was handed the reins on a caretaker basis. "It's always hard if you are the caretaker as any incoming manager will understandably want his own guys beside him. I just had to do my best and hope to get the results that might persuade them to give me the post on a permanent basis," said Scott.

However, his stint in charge got off to a difficult start. During a head tennis game after training, he felt a sharp pain in his calf and collapsed in agony. "I just went down as if I had been shot," he recalled. "Our physio Stuart Collie immediately diagnosed a ruptured Achilles tendon but, perhaps jokingly, Kevin McAllister told them to 'hurry things along as there's a game going on here' or words to that effect!" So for his first game in charge against a Rangers team on their way to a ninth successive title win at Easter Road on October 12th, Jocky Scott had the discomfort of having his leg in plaster.

It proved a dramatic afternoon, for despite falling behind to an early strike by Jorg Albertz, a Darren Jackson penalty and another close-in goal by Graham Donald put Hibs 2-1 ahead. In the dying minutes, Brian Laudrup hit the bar after Rangers were awarded a penalty but to the fury of the home support, the referee ordered a retake for an infringement. Up stepped Laudrup again only for Jim Leighton to hurl himself across goal to save before blocking another effort from the rebound - and Hibs held on to win!

"That was an exciting finale to a great game and I have to say that Jim Leighton was a magnificent goalkeeper for Hibernian. He made around 300 appearances for Aberdeen, joined Alex Ferguson at Manchester United then fell out of favour before joining Dundee in 1992. Simon Stainrod claimed he had a problem clearing pass-backs which I couldn't see but their loss was our gain. He came here, missed only one game in four seasons, deservedly regained his place in the Scotland team and went on to become the most-capped Scottish goalkeeper, second only to Kenny Dalglish with 91 caps.

However, there was a lack of stability in central defence. Much had been expected of Brian Welsh but instead the 26-year-old was plagued with a persistent Achilles tendon problem. Hibs had the experienced but aging Andy Millen and Joe McLaughlin but neither were totally convincing. And with Gordon Hunter struggling and Darren Dods not yet the finished article, the board gave Scott a vote of confidence by allowing him to sign John Hughes from Celtic for £200,000 in the hope of filling the void.

The rugged Hughes, who was from Leith, was also long on experience but he did the club and his manager a disservice by getting himself sent off in only his second game - a tough, tense derby against Hearts at Tynecastle. And although the Easter Road side managed a credible 0-0 draw, Scott's luck was not to last. With only one win from six games in December, he was sacked just before New Year and Jim Duffy, who had impressed at Dundee - twice taking them to the latter stages of the League Cup, was handed the manager's job.

"An assistant-manager is closely associated with the manager he works alongside, as it was with myself and Alex Miller, but that's not to say you agree on everything. So, when Alex left I relished the chance of doing things my way and found it incredibly frustrating at being judged and shown the door after just 13 weeks. I know things weren't perfect but there was a level of stability which, in my opinion, only needed tweaking. The board, though, obviously felt a fresh face and approach was the way ahead and appointed Jim Duffy, who'd done well on a limited budget at Dens Park. "Duff" was then an up and coming manager but in my opinion he made some radical changes which never really worked out."

At the time of Scott's departure, Hibs lay sixth but things were to get much worse. They ended the campaign in the play-off position and although surviving relegation with a 5-2 aggregate win over Airdrie, the decline continued throughout 1997-98. Duffy was sacked and despite the introduction of Alex McLeish, the club found themselves back in the First Division for the first time since 1981. Miller, like Scott, went on to have a varied career including two years as part-time assistant to Scotland boss Craig Brown, becoming assistant-manager at Coventry City alongside Gordon Strachan and proving himself a highly respected number two to Raphael Benitez at Liverpool.

There he played a key role in winning the UEFA Champions League in 2005, the UEFA Super Cup and then the FA Cup the following year. He also had spells managing in Japan, Sweden and Russia. Hibs fans, therefore, might reflect that their club had been overly hasty in dispensing with his services, and appreciate what he and Scott had brought to the club. Like Miller, Scott, too, would bounce back but in the meantime, it would involve a lengthy period of contemplation.

Chapter 13

Back Home

A t that stage, Jocky Scott might have been forgiven for letting his head go down. Between 1986 and 1991, his managerial career had been on an upward trajectory but since then, he had had a disastrous two years at Dunfermline, a flirtation with part-time football at Arbroath and the recent disappointment at Easter Road. "For around nine months after that, I had to work hard at keeping my spirits up and continue to believe in myself," said Scott. "I signed on the dole and sent out job applications galore but I had too much time on my hands and a lot of that was spent on the golf course. The Press had me linked with almost every managerial vacancy going but nothing transpired until I finally got a break in September 1997."

"The call came from Dundee United manager Tommy McLean, the former Rangers player and Jim McLean's younger brother - who offered me the position of first-team coach. I was glad to accept but with such great rivalry between the two Dundee clubs, and myself so closely associated with the Dark Blues, it felt strange driving past Dens Park to Tannadice every morning! But football is football, I needed to work and I was grateful for the opportunity to get back into the game at the top level."

"Like me, Jim McLean, with whom I was well acquainted from our earlier days at Dens, lived in Broughty Ferry. He had spent a remarkable 22 years as manager at Tannadice before moving "upstairs" in 1993 and, since then, Ivan Golac and Billy Kirkwood had held the reins with varying degrees of success. A year after winning the Scottish Cup in 1994, United were relegated, returning to finish third in the Premier League in '96/97 in Tommy's first season in charge, but they had struggled at the start of the '97/98 season before my arrival.

"It was good to work with experienced guys like Maurice Malpas and Dave Bowman - the latter became a close friend and golfing partner - the up-and-coming Steven Pressley and foreign talent like Sieb Dykstra, Kjell Olafsson and Erik Pedersen. The team did okay and reached the League Cup Final but, in February 1998, I again got the chance to manage in my own right. Local businessmen Peter and Jimmy Marr had been in control of Dundee Football Club for several months and they made contact via a third party to sound me out for the manager's job. My immediate response was that John McCormack was in charge and Dundee were top of the First Division but it appeared that they had a number of concerns at the way things were going."

On Saturday, February 7th, a 3-1 win at Stirling Albion put Dundee five points clear but within 48 hours, the unfortunate McCormack had been sacked and Jocky Scott appointed manager on a two-and-a-half year contract. The board and supporters had indeed been concerned at the team's dismal home record - just four wins from 12 games - with a disturbing habit of failing to see out matches and allowing the opposition back into contention. Unless the quality of performance and home results could be improved there was a genuine fear that things might come unstuck in visits to promotion rivals Falkirk and Raith Rovers late in the campaign - with fatal consequences.

McCormack, who had been Dundee skipper under Knox and Scott in '84/85, had been Jim Duffy's assistant before becoming manager in early 1997 but in *The Courier*, Peter Marr spelled out his reasons for the change: "We feel John McCormack has taken us as far as he could. He worked really hard, it's true, but in our opinion was not the man we needed for the longer-term structure we want to develop. By taking in a new face, an experienced professional with a good background in coaching at the top level at a time where he has got a couple of weeks before the next league game, we feel we are doing what is best for the club. Our prime objective has always been to gain promotion but we also need to be ready to compete at the top level

It was Jocky Scott's third spell at Dens Park and in *The Daily Record*, he commented: "We're top and it's important that we stay there. But I don't feel under any pressure and I hope I am not going to feel any. The players have done a good job up to now and I don't see why that should change. John McCormack has done a good job to get them there and I hope to continue that and improve things wherever I can. His departure is not a nice thing. It has happened to me before and I know how he must be feeling. But we are in a business where it happens all the time for different reasons. John's sacking was not my doing. I was offered a post and I am looking forward to it."

His appointment was welcomed by Dens central defender Brian Irvine who had spent three years under Scott at Aberdeen: "The other players were asking about Jocky after he was confirmed as manager and everything I had to say was positive. The happiest time in my Aberdeen career was when Jocky and Alex Smith were in charge at Pittodrie. We not only won the Scottish Cup and Skol Cup in '89/90, but also narrowly missed out on the Premier League title the following year. And having also seen him working at the SFA coaching school at Largs, I really believe Dundee are in the best of hands! Jocky himself has been generous in acknowledging the job John McCormack has done in taking us two-thirds of the way towards promotion. But now it's up to the new manager and ourselves to complete the task."

And complete it they would, though Scott's return began with a tricky Scottish Cup tie against Third Division Ross County at Victoria Park, Dingwall, where the Dark Blues emerged with a 1-1 draw. An awkward hurdle had been cleared and the job was completed when a 3-0 replay win set up a quarter-final clash against Premier League Champions Rangers. "That was a good start as confidence was the key. To that end, I brought in the veteran Hearts striker John Robertson on a month's loan and later signed former Aberdeen and Hibs midfielder Brian Grant. Both had been through it all before and had just the presence I wanted around the club as we entered the critical phase of the season," said Scott.

"I brought back Robbie Raeside who'd been out of favour and restored Eddie Annand alongside James Grady. Robbie, I felt, brought us more composure in central defence while Eddie, who'd been somewhat off the boil, gave us added power and movement up front. Anyway, we then won three league games on the trot, all by a single goal before going to Ibrox where the team acquitted themselves exceptionally well to get a no-scoring draw against what was a very good team."

"Although the game was live on SKY TV, there were over 40,000 there but experienced players like Brian Irvine at centre-half and Jim McInally in central midfield were immense and the others took their cue from them. We had around 3,000 fans behind us and they did us proud. It was probably the night, too, that goalkeeper Rab Douglas made his name as he withstood everything that Rangers could throw at him. We were slightly unfortunate to lose the replay 2-1 but the feel-good factor amongst players and fans was great and with eight league games left, we were ready for anyone."

The Dark Blues were on a roll and Scott's subtle tinkerings were in evidence as wins over Hamilton and Stirling Albion took them a couple of steps closer to title glory. "We had a 12-point lead over Raith and Falkirk but faced a tough finish with four of our remaining six games away from home at Broadwood, Stark's Park, Brockville and Love Street. First up were Alex MacDonald's Airdrie, who with fiercely competitive guys like Kenny Black, Jimmy Sandison as well as the creative Gary Mackay, were always a handful," said Scott. "We had to make sure we matched them for effort, so, I again put an extra man in central midfield, this time Brian Grant, and started with a 3-5-2 formation to see where that took us."

In the following day's *Scotland on Sunday*, Ron Mackay described the setting at Broadwood where Airdrie ground-shared with Clyde: "The playing surface had survived two late pitch inspections but, from the look of it - a soggy algaed pudding - it was not going to get through the 90 minutes without turning into one of those morasses which swallowed up cavalry and infantry at Passchendaele." In short, the pitch was a quagmire but although the battling Diamonds took the game to Dundee, the scoreline remained 1-1 until Jocky Scott threw on two late substitutes to try and win the game.

His job done, Grant was replaced by the lively Ian Anderson, with Annand making way for the physical presence of McCormick. It proved a master stroke for, with just four minutes to play, the winger's quickly-taken free-kick was driven across goal by Grady and the towering McCormick ghosted in net the winner. The changes breathed new life into Dundee and with other results going their way, a single point from their next game at Raith Rovers would clinch the league title and confirm their Premier League return.

This time, Scott opted for the attacking talents of Anderson as more than 7,000 fans, two-thirds of them backing Dundee, packed into Stark's Park. Paul Hartley put Raith ahead after 52 minutes but the Dark Blues moved up a gear and within six minutes, Eddie Annand rose to head home the equaliser to the delight of the travelling fans. It finished a goal apiece with players and fans celebrating noisily as a jubilant Jocky Scott confessed: "We had a few anxious moments near the end but our defence held firm. It maybe wasn't our best performance but it was a huge occasion for us and there were a lot of nerves out there. We showed how professional we are and are looking forward to returning to the top division. The support was fantastic throughout and that was great to see."

Now Scott had to prepare for life in the newly-formed Scottish Premier League or SPL which was the result of a breakaway from the Scottish Football League under whose auspices the "old" Premier League had operated. "It was great to know that Dundee were back amongst the elite - where we always should have been, in my opinion - and could look forward to visits to and from clubs such as Rangers, Celtic, Hearts, Aberdeen and Dundee United - though not Hibs who'd been relegated. However, once there, we wanted to establish ourselves and not become some sort of one-season wonder. I was happy enough with core players like Rab Douglas, Dariusz Adamczuk, Barry Smith, Brian Irvine, Ian Anderson, James Grady and Eddie Annand, but in the knowledge that more experience was needed, I signed Willie Falconer, Sean McSkimming, Tommy Coyne and Eric Garcin, who'd all been at Motherwell as well as Willie Miller of Hibs, either on free-transfers or freedom of contract.

An assistant-manager was also on the shopping list but despite speculation that ex-Dundee and Rangers midfielder John Brown might be the man, the more experienced Jimmy Bone got the nod. But after all the excitement of promotion, things didn't go well at the start of the campaign and it was almost mid-September before Dundee's first success, a 2-0 victory over Hearts at Tynecastle. "That got the monkey off our backs and was the start of a very good spell but although we managed five wins and four draws over the next three months, a couple of defeats was all it took to drag you back towards the bottom, said Scott."

"There was always going to be an initial period of adjustment. We'd gone from 3-5-2 to 4-4-2 and with Jim McInally and Brian Grant at the veteran stage, I promoted Gavin Rae from the reserves and switched Dariusz

Adamczuk to central midfield from his wing-back role. Dariusz was a gritty performer who was full of running and could score a few as well," said Scott. "He got both goals at Tynecastle and who could forget his lung-bursting run almost the length of McDiarmid Park to net against St Johnstone - incredible! He was a Polish international and very popular with the fans, who would chant: '*The Pole, the Pole, Dariusz the Pole. He gets the ball, he scores a goal, Dariusz the Pole!*'"

"However, we struggled from mid-December, a particularly bad spell which culminated in a two-nil defeat at bottom-of-the-league Dunfermline in March 1999. So after all the good work, we were within a few points of the bottom and bang in relegation bother. We'd taken a couple of real beatings, losing 6-1 to both Rangers and Celtic but although we knew we had to strengthen the side, we'd generally competed well. So, we had to learn from our mistakes, improve and just keep on going."

By then, too, other factors had come into play. All SPL clubs had to play at a 10,000 minimum all-seated stadium as well as having adequate pitch protection – and these had to be in place within a year of entering the league. To comply, the Dens board had approved plans for Barr Construction to build a new stand behind each goal but as this involved considerable financial commitment, the on-field slump had caused the board to seriously consider their position.

In February, it emerged that, under pressure by the SPL, there had been discussions with Dundee United about a merger of the two city clubs. And even after the fans vented their displeasure and rallied round financially, further talks were held before the idea - seen by many as a United takeover - was finally vetoed in mid-April. There were also suggestions of an investment by Anglo-Italian lawyer Giovanni di Stefano, an associate of suspected Serbian war criminal Arkan and whose clients included the notorious Iraqi president Saddam Hussein. This prompted widespread, negative media attention until the club severed their ties with him late that month. But even as those issues persisted, it was unclear if the board would give the go-ahead for reconstruction as time began to run out.

"The broadcast media and newspapers were awash with speculation about the stands, possible expulsion from the SPL and the other issues," recalled Scott. "So, yes, it was worrying but we could only concentrate on our side of things, which meant getting the best out of the players and obtaining the results to keep us in the SPL. We had a good group of players with Willie Falconer, Willie Miller and Shaun McSkimming of the newcomers doing particularly well but it was the signing of right-sided midfielder Steven Boyack from Rangers for just £25,000 that really helped us back on track."

"Steven was very direct and had the football brain to make things happen. His debut coincided in a 2-0 home win over Hearts, our fourth success against them that season and one that set us on our way to six wins from our final nine games!" It truly was an astonishing turnaround as the previously beleaguered Dark Blues went on to finish fifth, well clear of relegated Dunfermline and four places above Dundee United, courtesy of a six-game unbeaten run against Motherwell (a) 2-1, Rangers (h) 1-1, Kilmarnock (h) 2-1, Dundee United (a) 2-0, Aberdeen (a) 2-1 and Dunfermline (a) 3-1.

The win at Motherwell on April 10th meant that no fewer than six clubs were involved in the relegation struggle and with a much improved chance of staying up, Barrs were finally given the go-ahead. Within days, the demolition of the old Dens Park terracings began prior to the work on the new stands. And when the Dark Blues took the short walk to face city rivals Dundee United on May 1st, there was derby day glory as a headed goal by Brian Irvine and another by James Grady in the dying minutes secured a well merited victory!

That was sufficient to ensure Dundee's SPL survival as Jocky Scott recalled: "It was a fantastic afternoon and gloriously sunny, too! We'd done well against them, winning two - the other one when Grady lashed in his spectacular winner at Tannadice in November - and drawing one, the first derby, when we recovered from two goals down to draw 2-2 after a last-gasp Adamczuk header. That felt like a win as well, I can tell you!"

Scott had done a remarkable job in guiding Dundee to a fifth-place finish, their highest league position in 25 years, and he was a popular choice for the *Manager of the Month* award. "Keeping the players positive with so much negativity around was the hardest part but we came through it with a lot of credit and I was delighted for everyone after such an unsettling period."

"Actually, it wasn't so difficult motivating the players when the rest of the world - or at least the SPL - appeared to be against us! The off-field events just made us all the stronger with the players adopting a siege mentality," said Scott. "In the last half dozen games we played a more attacking 4-3-3 formation and showed that we were a really good footballing side as well."

Chapter 14

New Direction

Τhe recent completion of the two gleaming 3,000-seater stands had transformed Dens Park - if not completely - into a modern sports arena but hopes that the Dark Blues might continue their form from the end of the previous campaign were quickly dashed. "United got their revenge with an opening day win over us before we lost 4-3 to newly-promoted Hibs at Dens Park, said Scott." That was the first time many of our fans had seen the new stands which were named after two of the club's heroes from the 1962 championship winning side and they must have been impressed. The one at the TC Keay end was called the Bob Shankly stand after the manager, with the structure beside Provost Road adorned by the name of skipper Bobby Cox - with both set against the historic main stand on the north side of the stadium."

"It was a fine summer's evening, the pitch was lush and green so only the result spoiled a great occasion. However, it was always going to take us time to regroup after losing three of our best players. Brian Irvine, who was 34, opted to join Ross County who were able to offer a longer deal than us, while Dariusz Adamczuk and Ian Anderson departed on freedom-of-contract to Rangers and Toulouse, respectively. They were key men and, having received nothing in compensation, it was impossible to adequately replace them as the club was fully stretched financially."

It was late autumn before the side settled, recording three wins from four games against Hearts and St Johnstone at home, and away to SPL champions Rangers. At Ibrox, Dundee had led through an early Craig Ireland header before Rab Douglas further enhanced his fast-growing reputation with a penalty save from Jorg Albertz. Eventually, Rangers did equalise but with time running out, a clever Steven Boyack lay-off allowed Gavin Rae to race through and shoot low into the net for the winning goal.

"We were brave all over the pitch and although Rangers had most of the ball we played some nice stuff and attacked when we could," reflected Scott. "Now we need more consistency against lesser opposition." Unfortunately, without Adamczuk's drive and the flair of Scotland Under-21 international winger Anderson, the Dark Blues all too often showed a distinctive lack of punch and by early March 2000, had managed only one win from their next 12 league and cup games. This had included another early Scottish Cup exit to First Division opposition - this time Ayr United - as well as crushing defeats to both members of the Old Firm.

Rangers more than made up for Dundee's earlier coupon-bursting win by running riot in a 7-1 win at Dens Park. And when the Dark Blues crashed

6-2 to Celtic in Glasgow a few days later, Jocky Scott was under severe pressure. Home form had been particularly poor and when sections of the home support shouted abuse during the Rangers debacle, the Dens boss had responded with an angry gesture towards the main stand. "I shouldn't have done it and apologised after the game," recalled Scott. "Nobody enjoys getting a doing but although Rangers were brilliant we were second best all over the pitch and our defending was dreadful. I understood the supporters' reaction but I was every bit as frustrated," he added.

"Despite that, I still believed in my players. Rab Douglas was one of the best goalkeepers in Scotland, while Barry Smith was a stand-out in defence. By then, Lee Wilkie had made his first-team breakthrough and both he and Gavin Rae were in the Scotland Under-21 team. Willie Falconer could perform as a striker or at the back but we used him up front where his height and ability to bring others into play was invaluable. We'd signed Steven Tweed - who, like Willie Miller, I'd known from my time at Hibs - for £75,000 from Stoke City a year earlier. He was 6'4" tall, around the same as Rab Douglas, Willie Falconer, Lee Wilkie, Craig Ireland and Brian Irvine, and was an imposing figure in central defence."

Scott's conviction was justified when two of his "Old Guard" - Eddie Annand and James Grady - grabbed the goals in a late comeback to salvage a 2-2 draw at bottom club Kilmarnock. In a difficult week, Dundee's four-point cushion remained and that match was to prove something of a watershed. For Scott, though, there was added uncertainty. With just a few months of his contract remaining, the Dens boss had repeatedly requested clarification of his managerial future but now he received assistance in an unexpected way.

Dundee owner and chief executive Peter Marr, then resident in Majorca, had taken a keen interest in how Spanish football clubs operated and six months earlier, the club had appointed Voya Novakovic, a London-based football agent, as director of football. He, Scott was told, would help source players for the club "But," said the Dens boss, "I wasn't impressed. I felt his knowledge of what was required for the Scottish game was minimal and he didn't last long, about five weeks I think."

"We already had one Italian, Patrizio Billio, a midfielder who'd previously been at Crystal Palace. We had received an agent's letter and his CV by post, I asked him to come and train with us for a few days and signed him. He was a good player. In November, Peter had outlined his plan to me, telling me he wanted us to operate on the lines of Real Mallorca who'd brought in a number of South American players and sold them on at a big profit without weakening the team too much. However, due to our winter weather, the style of football played here and the fact English clubs had largely stopped buying from our leagues, I wasn't confident of it working at Dundee."

In March, six new players were sent over by Steve Archibald, the former Aberdeen, Spurs and Barcelona striker-turned agent, at the behest of the Marrs. It was a practice then unheard of in Scottish football but one commonly used on the continent. "I wasn't happy and obviously would have preferred to identify signing targets myself," said Scott. "Three of them turned up at Dens one Monday morning, telling me they were there to sign for Dundee - the others came later. I phoned Peter to ask what was happening and was told the players were now ours. To be fair to Peter I was under no pressure to play them and was told that I could select them as I saw fit."

"Three had little or no first-team experience - Martin Hugo Prest was an Argentinian striker, Chris Coyne an Australian Under-23 international centre-half who'd been at West Ham and Barry Elliot a Scotland Under-21 international winger from Celtic. The others were Spanish. Jose Mesas, a centre-half, was not as good as what we had, but I have to say that the other two, Javier Artero, who was a real speed merchant down the right and Francisco "Paco" Luna, a real live-wire of a striker, were quality and I had no hesitation in playing them."

Artero was highly impressive in a 2-1 win over Hibs at Easter Road, with the dynamic Luna taking centre-stage as Dundee crushed Motherwell 4-1 at Dens then netting another to ensure a vital point against Celtic before 47,000 in Glasgow. The Spanish duo had helped transform Dundee and the feel-good factor continued with a decisive three-nil victory against Dundee United in the Dens Park derby on May 6th.

Artero, whose late winner at Aberdeen a few days earlier had ensured Dundee's SPL status, was again the hero. He had run the Tangerine outfit ragged with his strong running, though it had been two-goal Willie Falconer - Dundee's top scorer that season with 16 goals - and James Grady that got the goals that mattered.

The fans were ecstatic for, after months in the doldrums, the Dark Blues were on a high. It appeared a winning combination with the experienced Scott as manager in charge of a good group of players, enhanced by a handful of talented foreigners. But, by then rumours were rife that Scott and Bone were on their way out of Dens and less than 48 hours later, the pair were informed that their contracts were not to be renewed.

An official club statement read: "There is no doubt that both men have been instrumental in taking the club forward to the point where everyone's aspirations surpass mere Premier League survival. The decision not to proceed with the current management team is no reflection on the abilities of either man. Nor should it be interpreted that they had achieved all that they could for Dundee. The records of Jocky Scott and Jimmy Bone speak for themselves. But the unanimous decision of the board is that a change of direction at managerial level is the desired option."

A final-day win at Dens against bottom club Aberdeen - soon to contest the Scottish Cup Final but set to escape a relegation play-off as Falkirk's Brockville ground was deemed unfit for the SPL - would have secured a second successive fifth-place finish. But a surprisingly lack-lustre display in a two-nil reverse meant seventh position instead and a disappointing end to Scott's second sojourn as Dundee manager.

Scott and his assistant Jimmy Bone had handled their situation with great dignity but in an interview with *Courier Sport*, the Dens boss revealed: "I'm angry, frustrated and very disappointed with their decision not to renew our contracts. As far as I'm concerned, I've been sacked. That's football but in my opinion this could have been done weeks ago but wasn't and it became the worst-kept secret in Dundee."

By then, the Italian brothers Ivano and Dario Bonetti had been unveiled as Dundee's new management team, leaving many fans excited about the prospect of top-class continentals coming to Dens Park but sympathetic to the departing Scott and Bone who had done well under severe financial restraint and shown their mettle when provided with quality players for the final quarter. The new boss was already known to Scott who later revealed: "I had met Ivano Bonetti before we played United in December. We had a pre-match meal at Dens, walked down to Tannadice and after the team talk, Peter Marr introduced us saying he was up from England and wanted to take in our game. I may be wrong but on reflection I think Bonetti may have been up to see the players and surroundings with a view to becoming involved."

Ron Scott of *The Sunday Post* had his own view of things and after praising Scott for re-establishing Dundee in the Premier League, he highlighted the huge gamble the Marrs had taken in appointing a young, relatively untried manager who had little knowledge of the Scottish game: "I know the Dens board were unhappy at the way Scott's signings of Tommy Coyne and Eric Garcin worked out (Coyne was past his best while the Frenchman had been problematic). But with no money, free transfers were the only way forward at that time. Now money is to be made available, yet Scott is being denied the opportunity to spend it. Surely he earned the chance to remain at the helm after steering the club to calmer waters following the turmoil of the Ron Dixon era?"

"My first meeting with Ivano Bonetti the other day left more questions than answers," the journalist continued. "For him to suggest he can rival Rangers' millions with "strategy and tactics" appears naïve in the extreme. I accept he and his brother played under some of the best coaches of all time in Italy. But didn't John Barnes arrive at Celtic Park with similar credentials? Last time Scott left Dens Park to become co-manager of Aberdeen with Alex Smith, the then chairman Angus Cook replaced him with Dave Smith. That was another huge gamble and it backfired drastically. I just hope Scott's departure this time doesn't signal a similar scenario."

Chapter 15

A County Boy

After his latest departure from Dens Park, Jocky and his wife Elaine headed off to the sunny Californian city of Santa Barbara, which is commonly known as the American Riviera. "There we met up with Archie Knox and his wife Janice, with whom we'd become close friends, but we'd hardly settled in to our new surroundings when my mobile phone rang," explained Scott. "It was my agent telling me that Notts County needed a manager and would like to interview me the next day! And before I knew where I was, I was back on a plane heading for the UK."

"County were in the English Second Division but I believed it was a club with great potential as the city of Nottingham itself had a population of almost 300,000 with the same again in its hinterland. I was immediately impressed by the Meadow Lane stadium which I thought was tangible evidence of their ambition," said Scott. "The chairman was Derek Pavis, a local businessman who'd been there for 12 years and had initiated the redevelopment of their outdated ground to comply with Lord Taylor's recommendations after the Hillsborough crowd disaster in 1989. It had been transformed into a trim 20,300 capacity all-seater stadium, completed in 1994 with the main stand named after the chairman and the County Road stand called the Jimmy Sirrel stand after their legendary manager."

"However, the interview procedure was strange to say the least. I was handed an application form with a string of questions which I had to complete. It was surreal but the outcome was that I got the job," recalled Scott. "On starting at Meadow Lane, I was keen to bring in Jimmy Bone who'd done such a good job at Dens Park and who had experienced English football with Norwich City. But despite repeated efforts to persuade the chairman, I was told that Gary Brazil, who'd been County manager for a brief spell after Sam Allardyce left for Bolton in October 1999, would be my assistant."

"He'd previously been a coach, then assistant-manager and remained under contract so I suppose financially it made sense to retain him. It wasn't ideal but unfortunately I was stuck with it, said Scott." The 38-year-old Brazil had good experience of all four English divisions as well as the Conference. His clubs had included Sheffield United, Preston North End, Newcastle United, Fulham, and in his Craven Cottage days his manager had been the ubiquitous ex-Dundee boss Donald Mackay! But although that gave him something in common with Jocky Scott it was to prove an uncomfortable relationship between the pair.

Formed in 1862, Notts County FC - nicknamed the Magpies due to their distinctive black-and-white striped jerseys - were England's oldest club and one of the 12 founding members of The Football League which began in 1888. There was keen city rivalry between Notts County and Nottingham Forest, whose stadiums, Meadow Lane and the City Ground, faced each other across the River Trent. By the late 1950s - Forest won the FA Cup in 1959 - County had become the poor relations, a status further diminished by the arrival of the ebullient Brian Clough in 1975, his style of management taking Forest to a First Division Championship triumph, two European Cups and four League Cups before his retiral in 1993.

Few would dispute that Clough was one of football's most successful, out-spoken and often controversial characters but County had an equally charis-matic personality in Jimmy Sirrel, their manager from 1969 to 1987. Sirrel, a straight-talking Scotsman who'd spent most of his playing career down south after a post-war spell with Celtic, had taken County from the Fourth to the Second Division between 1971 and 1973. He then joined Sheffield United but later returned to complete a remarkable achievement by guiding the Meadow Lane club to the First Division in 1981.

"He was a character all right, well-liked and part of the fabric of Notts County Football Club," said Scott. "It seems that as well as being manager, he did everything - the laundry, cutting the grass and typing the team-sheets. "There was one story about Jimmy in the football magazine *WSC - When Saturday Comes*. He used to come in from his home village Burton Joyce on a regular basis to use the team bath. One day he fell asleep after having a shave, not realising that he had nicked his neck, and a youth-team player saw the ring of blood around his neck and ran into the office screaming: 'Oh my God! Jimmy's dead!'"

He wasn't of course but sadly to say, Sirrel did pass away from natural causes several years after Scott's arrival. The older Scot's efforts in the '80s had been in vain as demotion followed and County's roller-coaster existence continued. And despite another brief spell in the First Division in 1991-92 under Neil Warnock - a year before the advent of the new money-spinning Premier League - subsequent relegations saw them slip to the new Third Division before returning to their current level under Sam Allardyce in 1998.

Scott made considerable sacrifices and would work tirelessly in an effort to raise the famous old club from its slumbers. His wife and family remained in Broughty Ferry and after initially living in a hotel, the Aberdonian moved in to rented accommodation. "Again, it wasn't ideal but to be fair, people were most welcoming and Jimmy Sirrel, who still attended games, used to come in for a chat every week. He was a really fine man and far from being critical, he would always be there to offer encouragement whenever we had a bad result."

Jocky Scott burns up the track with other ex-Dons Billy Williamson, Jim Shirra and Billy Pirie in 1979. Fotopress

Dundee and Aberdeen before Jocky's Testimonial in May 1981. Back - Duncan Davidson, Ian Scanlon, Andy Dornan, Steve Morrison, Neil Simpson, George McGeachie, Stewart MacLaren, Brian Scrimgeour, Andy Geddes, Stewart McKimmie, Jim Murphy, Colin McGlashan. Front - Jim Leighton, Dougie Bell, Stuart Kennedy, Willie Garner, Andy Watson, Doug Rougvie, Willie Miller, Drew Jarvie, Jocky Scott, Andy Harrow, Joe Harper, Eric Sinclair, Les Barr, Cammy Fraser, Alan Blair, Bobby Glennie.

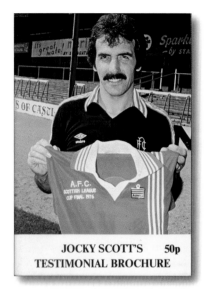

Jocky makes his point along with new Dundee boss Archie Knox when Scott was assistant-manger in 1984.

The great George Best in dark blue for a Dens Park Gala day in 1982 (from left) unknown, Tony Donald (Radio Tay), Ray Stephen, George Best, Jocky Scott, Dundee boss Donald Mackay and Dundee Rockets Ice Hockey star Chris Brinster.   Dave Martin Fotopress

Dundee FC 1986-87 with Scott in charge. (Back, left to right) Keith Wright, Stuart Rafferty, Stewart Forsyth, Jim Smith, John Brown, Graham Harvey, Alan Lawrence. Middle - Bert Slater (coach), Steve Campbell, Ian Angus, Tom Carson, Bobby Glennie, Bobby Geddes, George McGeachie, Ross Jack, Eric Ferguson (physio). Front - Jocky Scott (manager), Tosh McKinlay, Rab Shannon, Jim Duffy, Vince Mennie, Tommy Coyne, Drew Jarvie (assistant- manager). Dave Martin. Fotopress

The Dens boss rated Tommy Coyne his best-ever buy after signing him from city rivals United for £75,000. DC Thomson

Jocky Scott shakes hands with Dundee United boss and ex-Dens team-mate Jim McLean before another Dundee derby.

Pittodrie return as Jocky Scott becomes co-manager with Alex Smith in 1988. Drew Jarvie on the left completes the new-look Aberdeen management team.

Aberdeen Journals

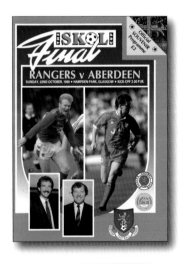

Evening Express

MONDAY MAY 14, 1990

SCOTTISH CUP WINNERS SOUVENIR

Dons in seventh heaven
SILVER DARLINGS

■ HOME ARE THE HEROES: and the city was out in force at the Town House   ■ WINNING COMBINATION: Theo and Brian with the famous trophy

Having beaten Rangers to win the League Cup, Aberdeen made it an '89/90 cup double by pipping Celtic in the Scottish Cup Final. Back (left to right) Alex McLeish, Hans Gillhaus, Theo Snelders, Robert Connor, Graham Watson, Brian Irvine, Stewart McKimmie. Front - Eoin Jess, Charlie Nicholas, Jim Bett, Paul Mason, David Robertson, Brian Grant.   SNS Group

Dunfermline Athletic 1991-92 (Back) Mark Bowes, Ian McParland, George O'Boyle, Andy Rhodes, Milos Drizic, John Hillcoat, Chris Sinclair, Tommy Wilson, John Reilly. Middle - Eddie Gallagher, Craig Robertson, Derek McWilliams, Istvan Kozma, Davie Moyes, Mark Haro, Andy Williamson, Raymond Sharp, Norman Kelly, Eddie Cunnington. Front - Ian McCall, Norrie McCathie, Pip Yeats (physio), Gordon Wallace (assistant-manager), Jocky Scott (manager), Jim Thomson (reserve coach), Joe Hudson, Billy Davies, Scott Leitch.

All smiles but Jocky Scott found things tough in his two years as Dunfermline manager. SNS Group

The Fife derby between Dunfermline Athletic and Raith Rovers was always a keenly contested affair.

Arbroath Football Club's Gayfield Park remains a trim little ground bordering the North Sea but Jocky Scott struggled to come to terms with managing the part-time "Red Lichties" in 1994.

Several familiar faces at the SFA coaching school in Largs. (Back row) Kenny Cameron, Dick Campbell, Jim Fleeting, Jocky Scott, Jimmy Bone, Jim Fallon, Jim Smith (physio). Front - Archie Knox, Alex Miller, Andy Roxburgh, Craig Brown, Alex Smith, Paul Hegarty.

Hibernian FC 1994-95. Back - Jimmy McLaughlin (coach), Willie Miller, Graeme Donald, Dave Beaumont, Keith Wright, Steven Tweed, Brian Hamilton, John Ritchie (community officer). Middle - Stuart Collie, Mark McGraw, Joe Tortolano, Michael O'Neill, Chris Reid, Jim Leighton, Graham Love, Davie Farrell, Chris Jackson, Martin Ferguson (coach). Front - Jocky Scott (assistant-manager), Darren Jackson, Micky Weir, Gordon Hunter, Alex. Miller (manager), Graham Mitchell, Kevin McAllister, Gareth Evans, Donald Park (reserve-team coach).
Scotsman

Keith Wright was a scorer who brought out the best in his strike partners according to Scott. Scotsman

Jocky Scott returned to Dens Park as Dundee manager for a second time in February 1998. SNS Group

Celebrations as Scott's Dundee side clinch promotion to the SPL after a draw at Raith Rovers in April 1998 (back, left to right) Brian Irvine, Harry Hay (sprint coach), John Elliot, Dave Rogers, Russell Kelly, Rab Douglas, Darren Magee, Steve McCormick, Robbie Raeside, Craig Tully, Gavin Rae, Gavin Rae, Jerry O'Driscoll, Front - Lee Maddison, Jim McInally, Iain Anderson, Barry Smith, Eddie Annand, James Grady, Brian Grant, Dariusz Adamczuk. DC Thomson

Jocky leads Dundee to another Dens Park win and fifth in the SPL in 1999 - their highest finish in 25 years. Others are Billy Thomson, James Grady, Steven Tweed, Jimmy Bone, Harry Hay, Jamie Langfield and Jim McInally. SNS Group

Notts County Football Club 2001-02 (Back, left to right) Henrik Jorgensen, John McCaig, Ian Baraclough, Craig Ireland, Stuart Garden, Steve Mildenhall, Saul Deeney, Leam Richardson, Mark Warren, Marcel Cas, Nick Fenton. Middle - Alan Travis (physio), Richard Liburd, Ian Hamilton, Tony Hackworth, Mark Stallard, Danny Allsopp, Niall MacNamara, Richard Holmes, Paul Bolland, John Gaunt (youth coach). Front - Gary Brazil (assistant-manager, Ryan Ford, Michael Brough, Gary Owers, Jocky Scott (manager), Darren Caskey, Kevin Nicholson, Paul Heffernan, Peter Fox (goalkeeper coach).

County's Meadow Lane stadium is awash and the pitch deemed a danger to health after the nearby River Trent flooded in November 2000.

Jocky Scott had only a brief spell as Raith Rovers boss but enjoyed his time there with Nacho Novo (right) an outstanding talent up front.

RAITH ROVERS FOOTBALL CLUB

OFFICIAL MATCH PROGRAMME

£1.50

Raith Rovers F.C. v Ayr United F.C.
Bells League Division One.
Saturday 2nd Of March 2002. Kick Off 3pm.

Jocky's next post was as reserve-coach at English Premiership club Sunderland.

Prolific striker Kevin Phillips was a popular figure amongst supporters of the "Black Cats".

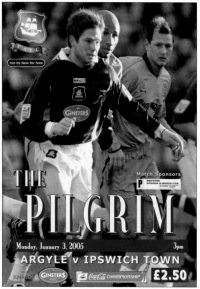

Next stop was Plymouth Argyle as assistant-manager to ex-Killie and Hibs boss Billy Williamson.

Former Dundee striker Steven Milne was one of several Scots on the Home Park playing staff at that time.

In August 2006 Jocky joined Tommy Moller-Neilsen as assistant head-coach at Danish Super League club FF Viborg but his continental experience was to prove all too short.

Back again! Jocky Scott became Dundee FC manager for a record third time in October 2008 with Ray Farningham returning as his assistant.
David Young Photography

Scott paid £180,000 for the talented Partick Thistle midfielder Gary Harkins.
David Young Photography

Another £115,000 went on the pacy Livingston striker Leigh Griffiths.
David Young Photography

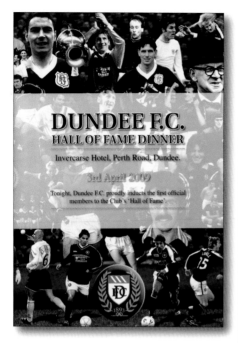

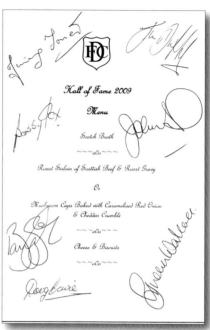

Right at home in his Dens Park office but players were devastated when Jocky Scott was sacked in March 2010.
Dave Martin Fotopress

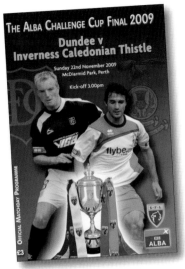

All smiles from Gary Harkins, Sean Higgins and Craig Forsyth but Jocky
Scott's half-time pep talk set Dundee on the road to victory.   Fotopress

Dundee beat Inverness Caley Thistle 3-2 in the final of the Alba Challenge Cup but the Highlanders won promotion to the SPL.
From left - Colin Cameron, Pat Clarke, Gary Harkins, Richie Hart, Eric Paton, Gary McKenzie, Sean Higgins, Leigh Griffiths,
Colin McMenamin, Derek Souter, Jim Lauchlan, Brian Kerr, Rab Douglas, Eddie Malone, Craig Forsyth.   David Young Photography

January 2011 Scott became manager of Stirling Abion but still had
time for advice to new Dens boss Barry Smith (inset). SNS/David Young

In Autumn 2012 Jocky rejoined Aberdeen as a coach and is pictured at an Under-19 game against Dundee along with
assistant-manager Archie Knox, Dons boss Craig Brown and chief scout Craig Robertson.   David Young Photography

Scott's English football sojourn began with a 1-0 win over Luton Town at Kenilworth Road only for Millwall to spoil his home debut with a last-gasp winner in a seven-goal thriller at Meadow Lane. The Londoners went on to win the league but Scott's side gained a measure of revenge with a 3-2 victory at the New Den on December 30th. "We had a decent squad and it was a case of improving things as we went along. In November we were fortunate enough to get Manchester City striker Danny Allsopp, an Australian Under-23 international striker, who was out of favour after earlier helping City up to the First Division."

"Danny initially came on loan but he linked well with Mark Stallard up front and after netting four goals in three games we paid City £300,000 to make the deal permanent. Both he and Stallard scored regularly and although there were other key men like our Welsh international goalkeeper Darren Ward, Gary Owers and Andy Hughes in midfield, we really upped our game after Allsopp's arrival. In the Ne'erday game we drew 2-2 with Stoke City before 9,125 at Meadow Lane, an attendance that was nearly double our average home gate. But although that lifted us to ninth, we were unable to sustain that surge and in the end, we finished eighth, though just six points adrift of a play-off place."

"Millwall and Rotherham went up automatically, Walsall joined them after winning the play-offs while Bristol Rovers were one of those relegated, having dropped a vital two points to us in September. There was a controversial finish to that game but there had been bad blood between the two clubs since a 1990 Leyland DAF Cup semi-final tie ended with rival fans fighting on the pitch after County had a late goal disallowed."

There had indeed been an explosive end to the more recent game at Meadow Lane with a furious Bristol Rovers boss Ian Holloway - more recently manager of Blackpool and Crystal Palace - demanding the match be replayed following an 88th-minute equaliser by Mark Stallard. That goal came after the Magpies failed to return the ball which Rovers, who had previously indulged in blatant time-wasting, had kicked into touch to allow treatment to the "injured" Steve Foster. After a few minutes the game resumed but County played on from the throw-in and the ball quickly broke to Stallard who scored, prompting furious protests.

With tensions running high, Marcus Bignott made a shocking tackle on throw-in taker Craig Ramage, who retaliated and was dismissed once the ensuing mass brawl between players had calmed down. At the final whistle Jocky Scott kept his players on the pitch to avoid any further confrontation in the tunnel, while Ian Holloway was eventually ordered onto the Rovers team coach by a police officer after a heated debate with a number of home fans. "I do feel some degree of sympathy for them," said Scott in his post-match interview with the *Nottingham Evening Post*.

"But, all I will say is that the lad went in for a 50-50 challenge with his feet and ended up rolling around holding his chest, make of that what you will. As far as Ramage is concerned, he made a rash decision and lashed out. But if he has to go then so does the other lad who was only booked, it was an awful challenge."

Later Scott added: "I'm not sure Foster was as badly injured as he made out. He was certainly one of the first players to chase after the referee when we scored. I think the fans in the County Road stand realised this and were baying for Craig not to give Rovers the ball back. Just a normal Saturday afternoon for us - but joking apart, there were further crowd problems in one of the following home games, against Brentford, I think, when a melee saw a linesman pushed by a player, and a steward got knocked out by a punch from a fan!"

"Then there was the great flood when the Trent burst its bank that November. Both the City Ground and Meadow Lane were affected with our pitch completely submerged and stands and offices also affected. Health and safety experts told us that the playing surface was contaminated with dangerous bacteria and that the club had to dig up and replace the entire pitch - an expensive business - and that meant our home FA Cup game against Gravesend & Northfleet had to be rescheduled for Gravesend."

"In the FA Cup, we travelled to Kent and beat non-league Gravesend & Northfleet, then defeated Dave Whelan's Wigan Athletic before eventually going out to Wimbledon. The FA Cup and especially travelling away to a non-league side was a great experience but one of the great things about English football is the geographical diversity. In our league there were Wrexham and Swansea from Wales, Bury and Wigan from Lancashire, Millwall, Luton Town and Brentford from London, the two Bristol clubs and a clutch of sides from the Midlands."

"It's refreshing that you only play each other twice in the league rather than four times as in the SPL. Then there's the incentive of reaching the play-offs and the excitement and extra revenue these generate both at the gate and from TV money. England, with a population of around 50 million has four senior leagues as well as the Conference so why Scotland needs a similar number of leagues with a population a tenth the size of England baffles me."

Without any previous experience of the English game, Jocky Scott could be well pleased with his efforts and now he looked to push for promotion in 2001-02. "I was happy with our progress but we lost a couple of good players on freedom of contract, including goalkeeper Darren Ward who joined Nottingham Forest. To replace him, we paid £150,000 for Swindon Town's Steve Mildenhall and spent another £120,000 on Leeds United striker Tony Hackworth as well as conducting a number of smaller deals. We brought in

Stuart Garden, the former Brechin and Forfar goalkeeper as backup - he was someone I knew pretty well as he was my son-in-law - and he gave County pretty good service over the next three years."

"We'd had Dundee central-defender Craig Ireland on loan since February and he'd done well too so we paid £50,000 to make the transfer permanent," said Scott. Scotland-Under-21 international centre-half Lee Wilkie was another player out of the picture at Dens Park. I'd given him his debut two years earlier and he was a great prospect but although I signed him for County on a three-month loan and he played a couple of games, things didn't work out for him here and he returned to Scotland a month early by mutual consent. He was not the player I worked with when I was Dundee manager."

"Lee was a good lad and I think that maybe concentrated his mind for he returned to Dens, got back into the team and went on to play for Scotland. Sadly, he suffered a cruciate ligament injury which badly curtailed his career. Overall, I'd say that County had a standard of player capable of competing in the lower half of the SPL and that their wage level was probably on a par with Dundee though one or two players earned a bit more," said Scott.

There was great optimism before the start of the 2001-02 campaign but Notts County made a disappointing start losing 4-2 at Port Vale, before there were wins over Cambridge United and Northampton Town and draws against Chesterfield, Wrexham and Brentford. "These drawn games left us off the pace," admitted Scott. "But in the League Cup we beat local rivals Mansfield Town then played Manchester City here at Meadow Lane on September 11th, 2000, the day of the terrorist attacks on the twin towers in New York. We led 2-1 but lost a late equaliser before going down 4-2 in extra-time to goals scored by their substitutes, Paul Dickov and Darren Huckerby."

The teams had lined up*: Notts County - Mildenhall; Warren, Baraclough, Fenton, Nicholson; Cas, Caskey, Owers, Grayson; Allsop, Stallard. Subs. - Hamilton, Hackworth, Bolland. Manchester City - Weaver; Pearce, Howey, Dunne, Tiatto; Grant, Berkovic, Colosimo, Horlock; Goater, Wanchope. Subs. - Shuker, Huckerby, Dickov.*

The Maine Road club had far greater resources than those of County but although Scott's side had excelled themselves, they were unable to replicate that level of performance in the league. After nine games they lay mid-table with increased criticism bordering on hostility directed towards the manager from sections of the volatile home support. At the end of September, Notts County suffered their heaviest defeat of the season, losing 4-1 to Oldham Athletic at Boundary Park, a result which saw them drop to fifteenth place.

Scott believed he could turn things around, but a dire display in a 1-0 home defeat by Wycombe Wanderers in early October saw emotions run high. "As I left the dug-out I was confronted by a fan who leant down from the main stand and gesticulated at me aggressively. Unfortunately, I took the bait and told him where to get off which didn't go down too well."

In need of a break, Scott headed north after the game, contemplating changes for the next match at high-flying Stoke City during the long drive back to Tayside. However, he would not have the opportunity to implement them for, on arriving back at Meadow Lane, he was summoned to club director Peter Storrie's office and dismissed. "The reason for my sacking I suspect had nothing to do with my performance as a coach, more to do with my behaviour in the dugout and an argument I'd had with the referee in the tunnel after the Wycombe game. Then, of course, my reaction to the supporter didn't help," recalled Scott.

For his part, Storrie had commented: "Unfortunately, Jocky's straight-forward management style and temperament increasingly conflicted with a more open relationship with others, from supporters and the media to the staff and board. A number of differences surfaced over the summer and during the first few weeks of the season. In spite of several impressive performances on the pitch, these differences in emphasis and style have persisted. We've agreed with Jocky that the most amicable way to resolve our disagreements is to part company." Referring to the appointment of Gary Brazil as head coach, he concluded: "We will rely on Gary for his inspiration and leadership to take us to the top of the Division Two table."

Scott made a point of saying goodbye to the players over a few beers but there was no love lost between Brazil and himself: "I was never really comfortable with him there and I think he was probably just as glad that I was being moved on. Let's just say the chemistry wasn't there. He wasn't my man and if you consider it from his point of view, I was the guy who'd got his job! A manager and his assistant should be a powerful pairing but in this instance the sum of the parts was probably less than the whole."

The inexperienced Gary Brazil was indeed appointed interim manager, only to oversee four defeats in five league games before he too was shown the door. And with County only just managing to avoid relegation and finishing sixth-bottom of the Second Division, the decision to axe Scott appeared rash. Due to his failing health Derek Pavis had sold his majority stake to Albert Scardino but remained as chairman alongside the American and his business partner, the former West Ham chief executive Peter Storrie.

Then, after persistent rumours that Notts County were in financial trouble, the club went into administration in June 2002 and consequently Jocky Scott who had only recently agreed to accept his pay-off in instalments, received virtually nothing in compensation.

Chapter 16

Travelling Man

So much for the beautiful game but this time Jocky Scott was not to remain in the soccer wilderness for long. "Towards the end of 2001, I got a call inviting me to Stark's Park in Kirkcaldy for a meeting with Raith Rovers chairman Dan Smith after the club parted company with their previous manager Peter Hetherston. It went well and I was given the post until the end of the 2001-02 campaign with the remit of keeping Raith in the First Division, Kenny Black remaining as my assistant."

Keeping them up would be no easy task as the Kirkcaldy outfit had struggled all season after flirting dangerously with relegation the year before. In the early '90s, Raith had built a good side under Jimmy Nicholl, winning the 1994 Scottish League Cup and achieving promotion to the Premier League for the second time in three seasons before having the audacity to take the lead in their UEFA Cup tie against the mighty Bayern Munich in Germany. However, the glory days were all too brief and when Nicholl departed to manage Millwall two years later, star men Stevie Crawford (Millwall), and Colin Cameron (Hearts), followed him out the door and by 1997, Raith again found themselves back in the First Division.

It was a situation that remained unchanged despite the endeavours of subsequent managers Tommy McLean, Ian Munro, Jimmy Nicholl (again), and Peter Hetherston. Over the decades, however, the club had produced its fair share of famous footballers, none more so than the brilliant Alex James, an inside-left whose trademark was his long, baggy shorts. James went on to star for Preston North End and later captained the great Arsenal side that dominated English football in the 1930s. But before then, in 1928, he had written himself into Scottish footballing folklore as one of the "Wembley Wizards", forming a formidable left-wing partnership with centre-forward Hughie Gallacher and outside-left Alan Morton, as Scotland recorded a never-to-be-forgotten 5-1 victory against the "Auld Enemy".

For much of the post-war era until 1970, Raith Rovers were an established First Division club with prolific goalscorers such as Willie Penman - their record scorer - and Gordon Wallace. In their 1950s heyday, it was the navy blue of Rovers that ruled the roost in Fife though not in as tangible a way as East Fife's three earlier League Cup successes. Back then, Raith could boast the famous half-back line of Andy Young, Willie McNaught and Andy Leigh, who between them made more than 1,700 appearances for Rovers.

No fewer than 657 of those had been by Scotland international central defender McNaught alone. And in addition to Willie Wallace who moved on to Hearts then Celtic where he won a European Cup winners' medal,

Raith had produced Jim Baxter, one of the most talented half-backs of his generation who went on to fame and fortune with Rangers and Scotland.

However, when Jocky Scott arrived, he found Raith Rovers rooted to the foot of an ultra-competitive league fighting for their survival with just 16 points from 19 games, though just a few points adrift of Ross County. "There were some decent players there, such as Senegalese international keeper Samuel Monin and Nacho Novo the Spanish striker who'd arrived on the back of a good scoring record with SD Huesca," he said. "Novo was then 22 and really pacy. He always gave 100% and was a big favourite with the fans, especially when he continued to find the back of the net with 22 goals in 38 appearances for Raith that season."

"Dundee signed him for £100,000, then after a couple of good years there, he joined Rangers for four times that amount and did really well," recalled Scott. "Up front, he was ably supported by ex-Airdrie and Dunfermline striker Andy Smith, who had a real physical presence as did big Shaun Dennis, who was back with his home-town club after four years at Hibs. Unfortunately, both were at the veteran stage and although they remained an influence along with Novo, Monin and stalwart defender Paul Browne, we just didn't have enough to give ourselves a chance."

"We had a good spell from late January to early March when we lost just one game from seven and at one point pulled ourselves off the bottom. We'd won at Clyde and had good home wins over St Mirren, Falkirk and top-of-the-table Partick Thistle," recalled Scott. On Saturday, February 16th, goals by Nacho Novo and Darren Henderson earned a 2-0 win over the Firhill side before a crowd of 2,800. The teams had lined up: *Raith Rovers - Monin; Millar, Dennis, Browne, Henderson R; Nanou, Davidson, Paquito, Henderson D; Smith, Novo. Subs. - McCulloch, Stein, Jones. Partick Thistle - Arthur; Craigan, Archibald, Paterson; McKinstry, Lennon, Hardie, Deas; Britton, McLean, Burns. Subs. - Roddie, Fleming, Walker.*

Unfortunately, they were unable to keep that run going and despite Scott's best efforts, Raith were doomed for the drop as they finished bottom, four points behind Falkirk who were spared relegation due to the demise of Airdrieonians. "The Raith Rovers job didn't last long and I left by mutual consent," said Scott. "Generally, managerial jobs crop up when teams are struggling and that was the case there. Sometimes increased fitness or a bit of adjustment to the team can do the trick or if funds are available you can bring in the missing ingredients. Alternately, when a lot needs done you need time to make the changes and with directors having to make a judgement, you sometimes just don't get that time."

"Nevertheless, Raith were a homely club and I enjoyed my time there. They are another of the traditional, mid-ranking clubs, have a good local support and are keen to maintain full-time football. Scottish football needs to pull out all the stops to ensure they have the stage on which to do so. Like Dundee, Partick Thistle, St Mirren and a number of other clubs, Rovers were compelled to build new stands to comply with the 10,000-seater stadia criteria stipulated by the Premier League only to find themselves in financial difficulty. I believe the league ought to have been expanded to absorb the clubs who had that sort of ambition."

"We used to train at Beveridge Park, a public amenity, just a short distance away from Raith's Stark's Park stadium. One day, I remember starting to set up an exercise by laying down markers to outline the area, when I noticed that the park attendant was right behind me picking them all up! Apparently we were not allowed on that part of the park grounds! It would have been good if we could have avoided the drop but unfortunately it wasn't to be."

The question now was, where next for Jocky Scott? The answer - Sunderland AFC and the Stadium of Light - was certainly not the most obvious. In the market for a coach, the recently appointed "Black Cats" boss Howard Wilkinson had contacted Craig Brown to ask his opinion about one particular candidate only for the former Scotland boss to respond: "I'll give you an even better option, a man with loads of experience in the game - Jocky Scott!" The Yorkshireman had great respect for Brown's judgement and immediately got in touch with Scott, who he invited to Sunderland for a couple of weeks in November 2002.

Wilkinson had a fine reputation, initially doing well at Notts County, where he had been mentored by none other than Jimmy Sirrel. He then managed Sheffield Wednesday before moving on to Leeds United, who he guided - with skipper Gordon Strachan and Eric Cantona as two of their star performers - to the English First Division Championship in 1992. Five years later, he became English Football Association Technical Director which led to two spells as caretaker-manager of the England international side, before he joined Sunderland when previous boss Peter Reid was dismissed a month before Scott's arrival.

The fortnight's "trial period" gave both parties a chance to take stock and in his first week, Scott worked with reserve-team coach Ricky Sbragia. But when the highly rated Scotsman then announced he was moving on to a similar position at Manchester United, Wilkinson, who had been impressed with Scott, immediately appointed him reserve-team coach. Jocky was understandably delighted: "It was great to get back into the game so quickly and with Sunderland then in the English Premiership, it was a bonus to join such a big club."

Sunderland, with their north-east rivalry against Newcastle United and Middlesborough, were indeed one of England's great old clubs and throughout the years, many a star footballer had worn the famous red and white stripes and black shorts. There were prolific scorers like Charlie

Buchan who had won the Military Medal in World War One and went on to edit his own football magazine - *Charles Buchan's Football Monthly* - and centre-forward Dave Halliday who averaged 40 goals a season over a four-year spell after signing from Dundee in the mid-1920s.

Other great names included inside-forwards Raich Carter (1930s), Len Shackleton (late '40s and '50s), the latter known as the "Clown Prince of Football" who cost the club a British record transfer fee of £20,500 from Newcastle in 1948 and Trevor Ford. Shackleton was a real favourite, endearing himself to the locals with comments like: "I'm not biased when it comes to Newcastle - I don't care who beats them!" He was a brilliant ball-player and one day with Sunderland leading Arsenal 2-1 and time running out, he went on a mazy dribble, put his foot on the ball and pretended to comb his hair while looking at his watch!

At other times, he reputedly mocked opposing full-backs by playing one-twos with the corner flag, sat on the ball to torment defenders who couldn't dispossess him and teased a beaten goalkeeper by putting his foot on the ball on the goal line - something that Scott himself would recall doing in one particular Dens Park derby! Back then, the Roker Park side attracted many of the best British players such as Northern Ireland forwards Johnny Crossan and Billy Bingham and of course the legendary Republic of Ireland international centre-half and skipper Charlie Hurley.

It was a club that was home to countless Scots including Neil Martin, Jim Baxter, George Mulhall, George Herd, Bobby Kerr and Nicky Sharkey in the '60s, with the combative Alex Rae, a future Dundee manager, playing there between 1996 and 2001. In the early 1960s Brian Clough netted an incredible 45 goals in 61 games before injury caused his premature retirement, while there was also the heroic goalkeeper Jimmy Montgomery who made a record 627 appearances in his 17 years at Sunderland.

Big-spending Sunderland, however, were relegated for the first time in 1958 and despite returning in the 1960s, they went down again. And it was as a Second Division club that they had won their last major trophy, when they defeated Don Revie's Leeds United 1-0 in the 1973 FA Cup Final, courtesy of former Raith Rovers left-half Ian Porterfield, who was destined to precede Jocky Scott as manager of Aberdeen.

Thereafter, it was a turbulent time for the Wearsiders, who alternated with dizzying frequency between First and Second Divisions. In the mid-1990s, former Everton and Manchester City midfielder Peter Reid took charge and, having achieved promotion to the new Premier League in 1996, he repeated the feat three years later. Between 2000 and 2002, Reid twice took them to seventh place but the '01/02 campaign had been a struggle with Sunderland finishing just one place above the relegation zone.

Peter Reid's response had been to institute a summer clearout before bringing in a host of new faces at a cost of over £16m. For years, the towering ex-Arsenal, Manchester City and Republic of Ireland target-man Niall Quinn and Kevin Phillips had provided a potent striking partnership. Three years earlier, the prolific Phillips had netted 30 Premiership goals to finish the highest league scorer in Europe and win the coveted European Golden Shoe. Last season, however, Sunderland's goals had dried up with just 28 from 38 league games and that goals draught was to continue into the new campaign.

Almost 36 years of age, the influential Quinn was past his best and that autumn he opted to hang up his boots. By then, Reid had paid a new Sunderland record fee of £6.75m to sign 6'4" tall Norwegian striker Tore Andre Flo, the former Chelsea player, from Rangers as a replacement. Other big money signings included Ipswich Town striker Marcus Stewart who cost £3.25m, Liverpool defender Stephen Wright - not to be confused with his former Aberdeen and Rangers namesake - for £3m, while a further £3.5m was spent on Leicester City winger Matt Piper, with the experienced ex-Liverpool central defender Phil Babb secured on a free transfer from Sporting Lisbon.

Babb apart, none would really live up to expectations. A less physical style of striker than Quinn, Flo struggled to form an effective partnership with Phillips. In contrast, Piper made an impressive start, only to suffer a succession of serious knee injuries which necessitated him having several operations and playing little over 20 games in his four years at the club. Wright too began well only for his form to deteriorate but although Stewart had a disappointing campaign, he at least fulfilled his promise by making good as a strike partner for the bustling Kevin Kyle - one of Jocky Scott's proteges - over the next couple of years.

However, that was of little consolation to Reid and with only two wins and a mere four goals from the opening nine league games, the under-fire manager was dismissed. In came Howard Wilkinson along with his assistant Steve Cotterill, who had quit his newly acquired position as manager of Stoke City to take the post. Little, though, was to change under the Yorkshireman who had inherited a bad hand and whose plans were further undermined by a catalogue of injuries.

As well as Piper, ex-Rangers and USA international Claudio Reyna - an energetic midfielder from whom much was hoped - would miss the rest of the season after suffering a cruciate ligament injury. Just as significantly, Danish international Thomas Sorensen - a dominating figure in goal - was out until January and with his understudy, Norwegian international Thomas Myhre also sidelined, Estonian national keeper Mart Poom was brought in on an emergency loan from Derby County. In the January transfer window that deal was made permanent at a cost of £2.5m though it was yet another international goalkeeper, the Austrian, Jürgen Macho, who featured most before Sorensen's return.

Plagued by injury and with results consistently going against them, this was a club in disarray by the time Jocky Scott arrived: "My position was reserve-team coach but the club had a large first-team squad of around 30 players and I worked with them from time to time. How the first-team performs affects everyone at a football club - there's no getting away from that. The English Premiership is an unforgiving place and I sympathised with Howard at the way things went. If you look at the make-up of his side at Leeds, you'll realise that he knew how to put a team together. But he never really got the chance to do that there."

A few weeks earlier, draws at Bolton Wanderers and Charlton Athletic were followed by a much-needed 2-0 home win over Tottenham Hotspur after goals by Tore Andre Flo and Kevin Phillips. However, hopes of continuing that run were dashed with the next four games yielding just a single point before Gerard Houllier's Liverpool came calling on December 15th. The teams lined up: *Sunderland - Macho; Wright, Babb, Bjorklund, McCartney; Thirlwell, McCann, Kilbane, Gray; Flo, Phillips. Subs. - Proctor, Stewart, Bellion. Liverpool - Kirkland; Carragher, Biscan, Henchoz, Traore; Murphy, Hamann, Gerrard, Smicer; Owen, Baros. Subs.- Diouf, Riise, Diao.*

Despite their lack of success, huge crowds had continued to flock to the Stadium of Light and there was a crowd of 37,118 for the visit of the Anfield Reds. In 68 minutes, Milan Baros struck for the Merseysiders to cancel out a first-half goal from Gavin McCann, who later missed a penalty. However, Sunderland were not to be denied and with just five minutes left, Michael Proctor, who had earlier stepped off the bench, fired home the winner to - temporarily at least - lift the Wearsiders out of the relegation zone.

But there was to be no revival. With the budget blown, little could be done in the January window and the pattern remained unchanged. A place in the FA Cup sixth round - the last eight - appeared there for the taking after Sunderland eliminated Bolton Wanderers and Blackburn Rovers but things again turned sour when Championship outfit Watford departed from the north-east with the only goal of the game. Finally, after just five months in charge and a run of 11 league games without a win, Wilkinson was sacked to be replaced by former Republic of Ireland manager Mick McCarthy in early March 2003.

By then, relegation was almost certain and with the newcomer unable to stop the slide, the campaign ended with nine straight defeats for a Premier-ship record low of 19 points as Sunderland crashed into the Championship. McCarthy - a Yorkshireman like his predecessor - remained manager but with the club carrying some £40m of debt after committing to fees and wages they could not afford, several top performers were offloaded at bargain prices to try to ease the financial situation.

Sorenson went to Aston Villa for £2m, Reyna to Manchester City for £1.45m with Kevin Phillips, scorer of 208 goals in six years for the Black Cats, departing to Southampton for £3.25m. Over the next two years, McCarthy took Sunderland as far as the play-offs before securing promotion in 2005. By then, Cotterill had departed to become Burnley boss, Scott had also moved on and McCarthy himself was dismissed a year later as he struggled to re-establish the club in the top division.

For Scott, though, involvement in the Premiership had been an illuminating experience. "I attended most of the games as the reserve fixtures were played at a different time. It was great to visit some of the famous old grounds although I had been to many before. It was the last season Manchester City would play at Maine Road and three years later Arsenal would leave Highbury for their new Emirates stadium. Manchester United, the champs, and Arsenal, the FA Cup winners, were far and away the best teams with United featuring David Beckham, Ryan Giggs, Paul Scholes, Ruud van Nistelroy with the Gunners' top men Thierry Henri, Patrick Vieira, Dennis Bergkamp and Ashley Cole."

"The training facilities in England were much better than the Scottish ones I'd experienced at Dundee, Aberdeen, Hibs, Dunfermline and Raith Rovers," he said. "At Notts County, we changed at our Meadow Lane Stadium before travelling by coach to the training ground at the University playing fields. Sunderland, though, was literally in a different league and in 1997, they moved from their famous old ground, Roker Park, to the new 42,000-capacity Stadium of Light and then decided to build their Academy."

"In my first six months there, we used a training ground consisting of three pitches with a big hut for a gym and portacabins for changing rooms before the new Academy was built at a cost of around £15 million. It was a state-of-the-art complex with at least ten full size pitches as well as a gym and a swimming pool complete with steam-room, sauna and Jacuzzi. There were various offices, treatment rooms, a boardroom, eight changing rooms with separate changing facilities for players and staff, and also a games room with over a dozen computers in it!"

For the next season and a half, Scott continued to work diligently with the reserve squad, though a change in the financial structure meant a drastic reduction in squad numbers, which left him only a few players to work with. "When I first arrived, it was enjoyable and my reserve side won the Premier Reserve League North. But once the squad numbers were reduced, it became really frustrating. I also missed the buzz of first-team involvement but out of the blue came an offer to move to the south coast with Championship club Plymouth Argyle in November 2004."

Ex-Kilmarnock and Hibs boss Bobby Williamson had been manager for the past seven months, a victory in his first game in charge leading to promotion from League One. And when defensive coach John Blackley, the former Hibs defender, moved on and Scott was offered the vacant assistant-manager's position, he was happy to make the move: "I was excited to be involved again at first-team level but on reflection I just had no idea just how far away and relatively remote Plymouth actually was!"

"Plymouth, with a population of around 250,000 had decent potential. Argyle had an average attendance of 14,000, well in excess of most SPL clubs and the wage structure was on a par with the bigger Scottish clubs except for the Old Firm. Facilities were decent too. The ground, main stand apart, had recently been redeveloped and adjacent to it, they had two training pitches, one of which was used by the youths."

For Scott, though, Home Park was to prove something of a home from home with a strong Scottish influence in evidence. In fact, former Rangers striker Bobby Williamson was the seventh Scottish manager in Argyle's history, the three most recent being former Scotland international defender Bobby Moncur (1981-82), Dave Smith (1984-88) - prior to replacing Scott at Dens Park - and former Dundee United and Scotland striker Paul Sturrock (2000-04), who had moved on to Premiership outfit Southampton in March after a highly successful spell with "The Pilgrims".

As well as Williamson and Scott, Gerry McCabe, who had been assistant to Williamson at his previous two clubs, was on the coaching staff while Argyle had recently signed the Scots trio of Motherwell midfielder Keith Lasley and strike pair Steven Milne (Dundee), and Scotland international Stevie Crawford to augment Marino Keith (ex-Dundee United and Falkirk), and Blair Sturrock, the son of the former manager. In addition. Matthias Doumbe (Hibs), and former Hearts midfielder Lee Makel (Livingston), had also just arrived from Scottish football to join former St Johnstone striker Nathan Lowndes.

Indeed, before the start of that season some fans had jokingly suggested that such was the Scottish influence that Argyle would finish middle of the Scottish Premier League! The Pilgrims - along with Yeovil one of only two English professional clubs to play in green - had had some decent results, particularly at home and on Boxing Day, 2004, goals by Wotton and Evans earned a 2-1 win against Ian Holloway's Queens Park Rangers before 19,535 at Home Park.

That day, the opposing teams had lined up: *Plymouth Argyle - Larrieu; Connolly, Doumbe, Coughlan, Gilbert; Gudjonnsson, Wotton, Friio, Capaldi; Keith, Evans. Subs. - Crawford, Lasley. Queens Park Rangers - Day; Bignot, Santos, Shittu, Padula; Rowlands, Miller, Bircham, Cook, Furlong, Gallen. Subs. - Best, Ainsworth, Edgehill.*

"In season 2004-05, we did well to keep Plymouth up despite vying with clubs like West Ham, Leeds United, Wolves and QPR, and finished seventeenth in what was a highly competitive 24-team league. I'd looked forward to re-aquainting myself with Steven Milne who had developed into a very good striker since I'd managed him as a youngster at Dens. However, he struggled to get into the side then got an injury which kept him out for months before he returned to Scotland to do well at St Johnstone. Stevie Crawford, too, struggled and also returned north to Dundee United."

"In my second season there, we began with a 2-1 win at the Madejski Stadium against Reading - their only home defeat on their road to the Premiership - but we then managed just a single point from games against Watford (h) 3-3, Derby County (h) 0-2, Crystal Palace (a) 0-1, Hull City (h) 0-1 and Brighton (a) 0-2."

"That wasn't great but although we hoped to get the time to turn things around, Bobby was summoned to the boardroom during a reserve game we'd been watching and returned to say he had been sacked. That was in early September 2005, and although I remained in a caretaker role for another few weeks, Tony Pulis was appointed manager and I then followed Bobby out of the door!"

Chapter 17

Denmark and Dens again

O nce again it was back to the golf course for Jocky Scott as there appeared to be little opportunity for experienced coaches in either Scotland or England. "It was frustrating but just seemed to be a sign of the times with many clubs going for young coaches, some of whom had just stopped playing. And for the first time I worried about ever getting back into football, he recalled."

In fact, it would be almost ten long months before Scott was again involved in the game and this time - August 2006 - his destination was Denmark in mainland Europe. He had been "head-hunted" by Danish Super League club Viborg FF's head coach Tommy Moller Neilson, who had been first-team coach at Rangers from 1997 to 2000 and had also spent a year as Ebbe Skovdahl's number two at Aberdeen.

After returning to Denmark to coach Boldklubben 1909, Moller Nielsen became Ove Christensen's assistant at Viborg in 2006. There he replaced Flemming Neilsen, who had been promoted to sporting director above Christenson, a move that prompted Christensen's departure and saw Moller Nielsen, then 45, elevated to head coach. "He was on the lookout for an assistant and when he contacted Archie Knox who had been on the coaching staff at Ibrox at the same time, Archie recommended me," smiled Scott, "And when Tommy phoned, I jumped at the opportunity to join him as Viborg assistant-coach."

But though greatly excited about his new challenge in Denmark, Scott would - as he had been at Notts County, Sunderland and Plymouth - again be living away on his own. "When I began coaching in England, I stayed alone in a flat and greatly missed my wife Elaine, family and friends as well as the home comforts which you take for granted. At Sunderland, I was only a few hours' drive away from home but getting home from Scandinavia wasn't such a straightforward option!"

"However, I had also spoken to former Dundee FC team-mate Hugh Robertson, who went to Denmark to coach Herfolge Boldklub in 1981. Back then, playing or coaching abroad was a novel concept and of course it was his departure which opened the way for my own coaching career at Dens. Shug took Herfolge from the Third Division into the top flight before returning to Scotland two years later. But he told me that he'd enjoyed his time there and that was a factor in my decision to join Viborg - from whom, incidentally, Finn Dossing joined Dundee United back in 1964."

So how had Jocky found life in Denmark? "The country itself consists of a peninsula and hundreds of islands and is just over half the area of Scotland.

At around 5 million, the total population is near enough the same as ours with Viborg itself – some 90,000 inhabitants - situated in central Denmark. However, unlike Scotland, the landscape is very flat and no location lies further than 32 miles from the coast," observed Scott. "The cost of living was quite high but it was a good place to live with an informal, relaxed atmosphere, very much based on family and friends and a slower more sedate pace of life compared with many parts of the UK."

"As regards football, the game's the same wherever you go and it was great to be working with good players again. The Danes have a 12-club Superliga with each club playing the others three times - home and away with the venue for the third game dependent on the previous year's position. The season in Denmark begins in August, they have a winter break from December until March, and then the league continues until the end of May. The club had a modern 9,566 all-seated stadium with gates averaging around 7,500. The standard was decent and probably the top four could compete comfortably in the SPL. Interestingly, though, unlike the SPL, two teams are relegated and two come up from the First Division each season."

However, his spell in Danish football proved short-lived and by Christmas, Scott was on his way back to Scotland. Results had been mixed and with Viborg battling near the foot of the table, former Swedish international Anders Linderoth was parachuted in as head coach. Tommy Moller Neilsen would remain, albeit demoted to assistant-manager meaning there was no longer a position for Scott. In an interview for *The Scotsman*, Scott declared himself philosophic about the unexpected turn of events: "These things happen in football and perfectly illustrate the perilous position of football managers. However, it was really disappointing as I was enjoying working in a new country. I can tell you that all the players understood English, although whether or not they understood me was probably open to debate!"

It was hardly a festive season of good cheer for the veteran coach: "It was nice to return home though it would have been much better to have had a position to go back to. I needed to work and applied for every coaching job going, no matter where in the world it was," Jocky recalled, but seemingly he was a forgotten man. Back in the UK, there continued to be a dearth of job opportunities and when something did come up, Scott suspected he was being overlooked due to his age and fretted that perhaps his managerial career was at end.

"Eventually, I accepted the post of Youth Initiative Monitoring Officer with the SFA though I really missed the day to day involvement of managing or coaching a full-time club. The SFA job was created when they introduced a Youth Initiative Programme which put all the senior clubs with Youth Development Schemes - age groups ranged from Under-11s to U/16s and U/17s - into two divisions depending on criteria. For example, at these age levels, teams trained two or three times per week depending on which initiative league they were in."

"My job was to visit as many training sessions as possible and check that everything was in place according to criteria. I had to ensure the correct number of coaches were in attendance, check their qualifications and monitor the quality and content of the coaching being conducted. I would then go to games, write reports for the SFA and attend monthly meetings to provide updates. The job was interesting and gave me great insight into how players were developing throughout the country. But, much as I enjoyed the job, it wasn't the same as a daily involvement with players and preparing them for a game at the weekend.

It was late October 2008 before Scott returned to football management and once again it was as manager of Dundee Football Club. This was his third time in charge at Dens Park and, having returned briefly to coach the strikers and youths in 2006, it was his fifth spell with the Dark Blues. Scott, who was then 60 years old, had signed an 18-month contract and in an interview with *BBC Sport* he told how thrilled he was to return to his spiritual home: "I've been trying for at least two years to get back into the game in Scotland. Everybody seems to think it's a young man's game these days, to the detriment of experience. But I've still got faith in my ability."

"It has been a long time coming since the last time at Dundee, but I am looking forward to the challenge. It left a bitter taste because I thought I had done well the last time and established the club in the SPL. Dundee Football Club should be in the Premier League and I hope that, before I leave here again, we are back in the Premier League."

Since Scott's departure in May 2000, it had been story of boom and bust with four different managers - Ivano Bonetti until 2002, Jim Duffy 2002 to 2005, Alan Kernaghan 2005 to 2006, and Alex Rae 2006 to 2008 - taking charge but failing to prevent Dundee going into decline. Under Bonetti, lavish amounts were outlaid on countless continentals including big names like Claudio Caniggia and Fabian Caballero, (Argentina), Georgi Nemsadze and Temuri Ketsbaia, (Georgia), and Italian striker Fabrizio Ravenelli. The plan had been to improve the team and increase income through gate receipts, then sell on the best players to fund replacements and continue the process. However, results were disappointing and the gamble had failed.

Good money was received for Caniggia but the 1995 Freedom of Contract ruling made many clubs reluctant to pay transfer fees and increasingly players were signed on pre-contract agreements. Dundee were unfortunate that the highly rated Caballero suffered a serious injury while Georgian international Zurab Khizanishvili joined Rangers without recompense apparently due to a registration error. But too many players had not provided value for money. There was style but too little end product and only Jim

Duffy's arrival led to a more pragmatic and successful spell which saw Dundee contest the 2003 Scottish Cup Final. That brought a long-awaited return to European football but, by then, national newspapers were reporting that the club's liabilities topped £22 million and Dundee FC went into voluntary administration to avoid the very real prospect of liquidation.

A total of 25 players and staff had lost their jobs and although Dundee managed to exit administration within six months, continuing cuts saw a much-weakened team suffer relegation on the final day of season 2004-2005. Duffy would pay the price with his job and his successor, the former Northern Ireland international Alan Kernaghan, lasted a dismal seven months before Alex Rae took charge in August 2006.

Alex Rae's only previous coaching experience had been with Rangers Under-14s. But although the board suggested Jocky Scott - then at Dens as a part-time coach - as his assistant, he opted for the far less experienced Davie Farrell, his friend. Scott, who had previously lost out to both Kernaghan and Rae for the manager's post, then had his position as coach terminated, receiving his P45 through the post without prior notification.

However, Rae did well to take the club to third, bettering that with the runners-up spot in season 2007 - 2008. But that was Dundee's third season "downstairs" and their repeated failure to regain SPL status prompted an exodus of promising youngsters like Kevin McDonald (to Burnley), Gavin Swankie, (St Johnstone), and Scott Robertson and Paul Dixon, (Dundee United). These were key players and their departure was a bitter blow. And when Dundee went seven games without a win to slip into the relegation zone, Rae and Farrell were sacked that autumn.

There had been speculation regarding names like Craig Brown, Archie Knox, Billy Davies and Terry Butcher - the last-named was assistant to Scotland national coach George Burley – but all were outwith Dundee's limited budget. Of around 40 applicants, only 20 were considered realistic and those were whittled down to a short list of five. The Dens board then suffered a setback when first Queen of the South, then Airdrie United and Brechin City refused the Dark Blues permission to talk to their respective managers Gordon Chisholm, Kenny Black and Michael O'Neill.

Jocky Scott and Stephen Frail were the others in the frame but although Black appeared to be favourite, the board ended the uncertainty by naming Scott as their new manager. In an interview with *BBC Sport*, Dundee chairman Bob Brannan talked of his hunger for the post: "I have seldom met anyone with greater desire for a particular job than Jocky to be the manager of Dundee FC. He has a reputation as an outstanding coach, tactician and organiser as well as a remarkable network of contacts in the game. For him the club is unfinished business and that is a feeling clearly shared by many of our fans. Despite the manner in which his last stint at the club ended, he has never stopped believing in Dundee FC and, in turn, the board believe in him. That is why he is unquestionably the man for us."

Brannan had noted the immediate impact made by Harry Redknapp - Scott's former Seattle Sounders' team-mate who was also in his 60s - at struggling Tottenham Hotspur and, in *The Sunday Post*, Scott repeated his own views on the topic: "The trend is towards appointing guys who have just stopped playing. But, believe me, you need to serve your time before you are ready to step into football management. A lot of young managers at present don't go about the job the way they should. I'll take training myself every day. I won't run about – because I can't! But I'll be out there working with the players. Age should not matter and ideally, I'll be able to groom my own successor. It will be good for Dundee to have a ready-made replacement when it's time for me to go again."

Ray Farningham had lost his coaching job at Dens following relegation in 2005 but now he became assistant-manager with the long-serving Barry Smith back as youth coach to the Under-19s. Both were regarded as "Dundee men" and Scott's concept of succession planning went down well with the fans. There was, however, no instant solution to the onfield problems with Scott's first game back in charge resulting in a 1-1 draw against his former Raith assistant Kenny Black's Airdrie United at Dens as the Dark Blues fielded: *Douglas; Pozniak, Benedictus, McKeown, Malone; Daquin, Williams, Mearns, O'Brien; Antoine-Curier, Deasley. Subs . - Gilhaney, Davidson. Airdrie United - Robertson; Smith D, McDonald, Lovering, Smith L; Nixon McKenna, Di Giacomo, Cardle; Lynch, McLaughlin. Subs. - McDougall, Brown, Noble.*

The new boss had sprung a surprise by handing 16-year-old Kyle Benedictus his debut at centre-half. The young Dundonian did well and further impressive performances gained him that month's *Irn-Bru Young Player of the Month* award as well as an extended contract. Prior to Scott's arrival, Dundee had taken just 12 points from their opening 11 games and looked more in danger of going down rather than up. However, the veteran boss began by introducing double training sessions and steadied the ship with a couple of wins and two draws to earn the accolade of the *Irn-Bru Phenomenal Manager of the Month* for November.

Manager, board and fans still harboured hopes of promotion and when Derek McInnes' table-topping St Johnstone came to Dens, around 6,500 fans turned out to see a thrilling encounter end 1-1, leading Scott to say: "The fact our crowd against Saints was higher than three games in the SPL shows there is a ready audience here. I've no doubt there is little or nothing between the top sides in our division and most of the teams in the SPL. I don't know anything about the prospects of SPL 2 but I'm sure both clubs could survive in a bigger SPL."

The Scott influence was there for all to see as big goalkeeper Rab Douglas, back at Dens after eight years at Celtic and Leicester City, remarked: "Jocky is doing his utmost to get the best out of the players at his disposal. We are definitely more organised and tactically aware, everyone knows what their job is and there is a great spirit about the place." In a move to freshen things up, the manager brought in two youngsters of real quality on loan deals from Rangers in attacking midfielder Andrew Shinnie, with whom he had worked while assisting the Scotland Under-19s, and the pacy Cypriot winger Giorgios Efrem.

A steady improvement saw Dundee narrow the leeway at the top to six points before the Tayside rivals met again at the end of February. But although some 3,000 Dundee supporters were amongst an expectant 7,000-plus crowd at Perth, the result was a no-scoring stalemate. Thereafter, the Dens Park promotion challenge stalled and the Dark Blues ended fourth behind runaway winners St Johnstone, Partick Thistle and Dunfermline. For although Dundee's defence was the best in the league, finding the net had been a real problem with a lack of strength and creativity in midfield and a dearth of firepower up front.

Scott was philosophic: "It was a big ask as the squad I inherited wasn't really good enough. We gave it our best shot and to actually be in the promotion mix until late in the season was about as good as it was going to get. For a while I believed we could do it but, having got ourselves into a decent position, we were unfortunate to lose Shinnie, Efrem and Antoine-Curier for a couple of matches due to international commitments and managed just one win from seven games in March and mid-April. Now I'm looking forward to building a squad for next season that is capable of getting the club out of this division and back to where we belong."

Chapter 18

Stick or Twist

Sometimes in football an event can occur which in sporting parlance is known as a "game-changer". The fabulously wealthy Roman Abramovich and Sheikh Mansour had taken control at Chelsea and Manchester City, respectively, and both English Premiership clubs were transformed. Now, in the spring of 2009, there was hope that Dundee FC, too, might have found their own home-grown benefactor in the shape of Calum Melville.

Earlier, Dundee had dismissed financial concerns raised by the club auditors although Bob Brannan, himself a wealthy man who had been chairman since the 2003 - 2004 administration, agreed that the four-man board required to be expanded and further investment was required. In a novel move, the club had placed an advert in *The Sunday Times* inviting applications from those with a business background keen to become involved in football. And when Melville, an Aberdeen-based oil executive, responded, he was co-opted on to the Dens Park board.

"I remember Bob Brannan telling me that exhaustive checks had been made and Calum Melville appeared to be an extremely wealthy man. His personal wealth, it was hoped, would go a long way to solving the club's financial problems," said Jocky Scott. However, Melville, a life-long Dons fan, who was listed in *The Sunday Times* top-500 "rich-list" and reckoned to be worth around £125m, insisted that Dundee would continue their prudent approach of the past few years.

Scott welcomed the news that he would get a 25% budget increase but recognised the responsibility and pressure that came with it. "Ray Farningham and I wanted to reduce the squad to 18 to 20 players, comprising three or four central defenders, a similar number of strikers with the others - like Eric Paton - able to do a job in a variety of roles. We knew the positions needing filled and the type of people for them but, most of all, we wanted guys of experience who were winners. Injury history was also a consideration," said Scott.

"We weren't scoring enough and either had to get more out of Antoine-Curier (who went to Hamilton on loan), McMenamin and young Brian Deasley or by providing a better service to them. We also needed fresh faces but although I'd always liked the hard running and powerful shooting of Queen of the South striker Stephen Dobbie, he joined Championship side Swansea City. I was keen on three players from Livingston, who were demoted to the Third Division after going into administration for a second time. But although we agreed to pay £75,000 for right-back Dave Mackay and midfielder Murray Davidson, they went to St Johnstone and, initially, it didn't look like we'd get Leigh Griffiths, their promising Scotland 'B' international striker who'd scored 23 goals that term, either."

"Calum Melville took a keen interest and started calling me daily about players he thought might be of interest. It was something I had to accept although managers are wary about directors who offer their advice on footballing matters," said Scott. "Since the days of Angus Cook, I've always been a bit dubious about press-hyped rich guys who get involved in football but it was Calum's financial backing that ensured Dundee were the only Scottish club apart from Celtic to splash out on transfer fees that summer."

In came 10 new players, many on 3-year deals, the pick of whom were Partick Thistle midfielders Gary Harkins - recently voted the First Division Player of the Year - for £150,000 with £115,000 required to prise Leigh Griffiths from Livingston. The others were midfielders Brian Kerr, a former Scotland international, and Richie Hart, on freedom of contract from Inverness Caledonian Thistle and Ross County, with ex-Motherwell and Slovakian defensive midfielder Maros Klimpl arriving from Danish football in September; likewise strikers Sean Higgins (Ross County) and Pat Clarke (Clyde), goalkeepers Tony Bullock (Montrose), and former Dundee United youth John Gibson (Dundee United), were signed as was right-back Chris Casement - freed by Ipswich - who had recently been capped by Northern Ireland.

Melville had been keen to buy back Dens Park Stadium - for an estimated £600k - from John Bennett, the former Dundee United director whose cash injection had helped Dundee free themselves from the post-administration shackles of the bank. That possibility foundered but the club's newest and most influential director had shown the financial muscle he felt necessary to propel Dundee back to the SPL, and with only the top team promoted, stressed: "Second is nowhere. After four years in the First Division, we simply have to get up!"

The '09/10 campaign began well for Scott's new-look side when a Sean Higgins' goal brought victory in the league opener against Morton at Dens. That provided a platform on which to build a sustained promotion challenge, but there were also moments of magic in the League Cup and the Alba Challenge Cup, with media interest going into overdrive when early League Cup successes against lower league sides set up a third-round clash with Melville's home-town team Aberdeen at Dens Park.

Goals by Malone and Forsyth put Dundee two goals up only for the Dons to pull level in the dying minutes. It looked as if their chance had gone but in extra-time a razor sharp Leigh Griffiths pounced on a Jamie Langfield blunder to roll in the winner. It was like old times, particularly when the quarter-final draw threw up another home tie, this time against Rangers.

There was a crowd of 10,654, the largest at Dens since the club had last been in the SPL, but although Griffiths again made his mark with a stunning free-kick to equalise, the Light Blues departed with a 3-1 win.

Discussing Griffiths in *The Sunday Post*, Scott had said: "It's up to Leigh to show he wants it enough to go right to the very top. He certainly has the ability. Despite his goals, he has a lot to learn but he has more than enough natural talent so if he marries the two, he could be some player. He's definitely got a lot going for him but we're still working on when it's right for him to be an individual and when to be part of the team."

Dundee, then, had impressed against SPL opposition and a continuation of that form left them with just one defeat in 11 games before they met Inverness Caledonian Thistle in the Challenge Cup Final in late November. The teams lined up: *Inverness Caley Thistle - Esson; Tokely, Bulvitis, Munro, Golabeck; Hayes, Proctor, Duncan, Sanchez; Foran, Rooney. Subs. - Cox, Imrie, Odhiambo. Dundee - Douglas; Paton, MacKenzie, Lauchlan, Malone; Harkins, Hart, Kerr, Forsyth; Higgins, Griffiths. Subs. - Benedictus, McMenamin, Clark.*

Dundee supporters travelled to McDiarmid Park in large numbers but early exuberance dissolved as a high-tempo approach by Terry Butcher's side left the shell-shocked Dens men two goals down at half-time. The Dark Blues had struggled but after the restart it was a different story. Within three minutes Bulvitis headed an own goal under pressure by Higgins and soon afterwards, Gary Harkins was on hand to sweep home the equaliser. The midfield maestro had also created the first goal and with seven minutes left, he was again involved when he cut the ball back for Craig Forsyth, son of accomplished Dundee defender Stewart Forsyth from the 1980's, to crash in the winner!

At the final whistle, there were scenes of jubilation but clearly there had been some straight talking at the interval: "It was right up there with the best of half-time rants," confirmed Jocky Scott. "And, yes, there were a few wee sweary words! I stressed the importance of the occasion, told the players they were letting everyone down and that they had to get back out and put in a huge effort if they were to win the trophy."

Scott's words had the desired effect and boosted by that result and the manner of their victory, Dundee went on to record four straight wins before taking a hard-earned point away to Inverness Caley Thistle to complete 2009 unbeaten in their previous 13 league games. The Melville master plan looked well on track, for, with the league programme just past the halfway stage, Dundee lay eight points ahead of Queen of the South and Ross County, with Partick Thistle just behind and Caley Thistle a massive 12 points in arrears.

Jocky Scott, though, had remained cautious: "Despite the press making us promotion favourites we weren't getting carried away. I stressed to the players that we had to take one game at a time though we were confident that we could continue our good form. Ross County and QOS have games in hand, which if they win, could put us under pressure. And after their dynamic first-half performance against us in Perth, there was no way I was discounting Caley Thistle."

Calum Melville, by then a high-profile figure, had adopted a populist approach, mixing with the ordinary supporters in the stands and declaring that he saw Dundee as a potentially bigger club than city rivals Dundee United. The success-starved fans bought into much of what he said but remarks made on *BBC Sportsound* that Dundee were keen to re-sign midfielder Scott Robertson from the Tannadice outfit in the January transfer window did not go down well across the road and earned Melville an SFA reprimand.

On January 2nd, Dundee's game against bottom of the league Airdrie United was switched from snowbound New Broomfield to Dens Park following an approach to the Scottish League. With undersoil heating at Dens, it was the only First Division game to go ahead that day but the move was to backfire as the Dark Blues - who were without the suspended Gary Harkins - lost to the only goal of the game. Talking to *The Courier* afterwards, a grim-faced Jocky Scott commented: "Everything that could go wrong today did go wrong, it's as simple as that. It's a shame because a lot of people worked very hard to ensure the match went ahead and after all that, we've let ourselves and the fans down."

It had been hoped that the game might bring out a good crowd, while a win would have put further pressure on the chasing pack. But on a freezing cold day, just over 4,000 turned up and conditions were to play their part in a disastrous day. The normally deadly Leigh Griffiths missed a penalty only for Airdrie to score with a disputed award at the other end before Gary MacKenzie was red-carded when he caught the visiting keeper with his studs in an ill-advised challenge. As the temperature fell and the playing surface deteriorated, Dundee were unable to play their normal passing game and the visitors held on to win.

That left Scott's men facing a glut of away games towards the end of the season but just as significantly, MacKenzie was hit by a three-game suspension affecting crucial clashes against Queen of the South and Ross County. The big ex-Ranger, who did not have the best of disciplinary records had forged a solid partnership with the experienced Jim Lauchlan in central defence but further news that he had turned down a three-year deal with Dundee to sign a pre-contract agreement for MK Dons - managed by former Dens boss Alex Rae - cast some doubt on his commitment to Dundee.

There was a creditable draw at Palmerston but a dismal display at Dens on January 30th saw Dundee dumped 1-0 by the dour men of Dingwall. As well as MacKenzie, 17-goal Leigh Griffiths was also an absentee but despite entering the fray as a half-time substitute, he was unable to affect the outcome. The loss of this "six-pointer" was a bitter blow leaving second-placed Ross County six points behind with three games less played. And with Caley Thistle and Queen of the South also closing in with games in hand, Jocky Scott knew the title race was heading for the wire.

Griffiths had been left out for disciplinary reasons as Scott explained: "It was such an important game and Leigh let us down. We knew before signing him that he had a bit of a bad-boy reputation off the field and I insisted he stay in Dundee and only return to Edinburgh at weekends after matches. But unknown to me he had gone home the night before the Ross County game and didn't report to Dens Park at 1.30 pm with the rest of the squad. It transpired he was stuck in traffic on the motorway and when he missed the 2.10 pm team talk, I omitted him from the starting X1."

"Leigh Griffiths and Gary Harkins were two of our top players with Harkins absolutely outstanding for me. He was a big powerful player, had brilliant close control and passing ability, could tackle and was good in the air, but best of all he could get us goals from midfield. Leigh was pacy, had a great shot and could get the goals but he wasn't the easiest to handle. He was still a young lad and when he first arrived was petulant if things didn't go right at training. Then on establishing himself he became cocky and resented criticism, but he did well for us before going off the boil a bit in the early part of 2010."

"We were going through a sticky spell and around that time I was invited to meet Calum Melville at his Aberdeen home. That was obviously a concern but he was really supportive and assured me that even if we didn't get promotion I would remain manager and could try again next season. I asked if the other directors felt the same and was told that that was not a worry, a reply which made me feel that he was the man calling the shots."

"In the next game we beat Partick Thistle but due to postponements it was early March before we played again, drawing 2-2 with Caley Thistle at Dens after battling back from two goals down. We'd blown another opportunity to distance ourselves from one of our closest challengers and following the recent deaths of Bobby Cox and Hugh Robertson of the 1962 League Championship winning side - both good friends from my first spell at Dens - these were difficult days for all associated with the club," said Scott.

"As well as promotion, we were looking for a good run in the Scottish Cup and having earlier seen off Livingston and Ayr United, we were confident of overcoming Raith Rovers in the Dens quarter-final on March 13th. A repeat of the urgency shown latterly against Caley Thistle was a must but instead we lost two dreadful goals from dead-ball situations in the first nine minutes. And although we got one back and dominated, we were unable to repair the damage."

Prior to this, the Dens boss had been the subject of criticism by fans on internet message boards and the day after the cup-tie, he was summoned to meet Bob Brannan at a hotel in Dundee: "The chairman was extremely agitated as the club had lost out on a £300,000 semi-final windfall and it appeared that I was to carry the can. So, despite my recent meeting with Melville, I felt under huge pressure and a 1-1 draw from our midweek trip to Ayr a few days later brought little relief although we'd actually played very well."

A win at Airdrie that Saturday was imperative but with Eric Paton and Leigh Griffiths suspended after being red-carded at Ayr, the depleted Dark Blues then lost Gary MacKenzie who was stretchered off with concussion in the opening minutes. "You just couldn't make it up but even then we did well enough until conceding a goal early in the second half. After that, things deteriorated and we went down 3-0 for our heaviest defeat of the season," said Scott. "Unfortunately, Rab Douglas conceded two bad goals after exacerbating a groin injury which he'd had for a few weeks and that was him out for the rest of the campaign."

On the coach back to Dundee, Scott received a text from Calum Melville indicating that they should meet at Dens Park: "He hadn't been at the game but having recently assured me that Ray and I would remain in charge, he felt it only right he should take the responsibility of telling me the bad news. He simply said that the board wanted a new manager and that was me and Ray out." Since the turn of the year, there had been just two wins from eight league games and an official club statement confirmed that the board had unanimously agreed that a change should be made "while there was still time for another manager to secure the victories necessary to get the team back to the SPL".

Within 24 hours, Queen of the South boss Gordon Chisholm was appointed manager with Billy Dodds, who had coached their forwards on a part-time basis, as his assistant. Chisholm, a former Dark Blue signed by Scott in 1987, had impressed in his three years with Queens, guiding them to the 2008 Scottish Cup Final, which they had narrowly lost to Rangers. It had been expected that his tough as teak assistant, Kenny Brannigan, would accompany him but instead Dodds, the former Dundee and Scotland striker, a man of many clubs and by then a BBC Scotland football pundit, was brought in.

It appeared to have been stick or twist as the Dens directors gambled on a new management team which they believed gave them a better chance of going up. But history would show that the move was doomed to failure, just two wins in the final quarter consigning Dundee to runners-up spot, 12 points behind Inverness Caley Thistle. It was a sad end to a campaign that had promised so much and the implications would be profound. The Calum

Melville gravy train appeared to have ground to a halt, and with the club having fallen into arrears with HMRC and with considerable financial commitments to players and management as well as the issue of compensation for Scott and Farningham, Dundee FC were in serious trouble.

Melville's comment in *The Courier* in April 2009 that "sustainability and stability are the key factors behind Dundee FC", now seemed a mere illusion and within four months, the club had entered administration for a second time with many of the players scathing about Scott's dismissal. In the book *It's All About the Memories* by Kenny Ross and Jacqui Robertson, Colin McMenamin - one of 13 players and staff to lose their jobs remarked: "The whole place died the day they sacked Jocky Scott and we just never recovered. The boys were so close to him and felt really let down by the board at the time."

That opinion was reinforced by Scott: "I believe it was a classic case of panic without considering the effect on morale. The players and staff were a tight bunch and to a man they felt we could recover and go on to win the league. Everyone had to hold their nerve but, sadly, in my opinion the board of directors did not."

"I wasn't that surprised things didn't go well under the new guys but I was disappointed at their comments about the players not being fit enough. It was untrue and totally disrespectful. It's easy to walk in and profess to have the answer to everything but quite another thing to deliver in terms of results. Anyway, regardless of what I thought, Ray and I were out - sacked, booted out when we were so close. Full credit to Caley Thistle, a very good side who went 21 games unbeaten to win the league but we still held a three point lead over them and Dunfermline when we left and I think we could have regrouped and put real pressure on them."

"It would have helped if we'd managed to strengthen the squad with a couple of experienced players in the January window as we'd had a number of players like Sean Higgins, Gary McKeown, Paul McHale, Maros Klimpl, Colin Cameron, Darren Young and David Cowan out with lengthy injuries. We got Andrew Shinnie back on loan from Rangers to bolster midfield but were keen to get in an experienced centre-half and a proven scorer. The Slovakian Milan Palenik wanted to return to Dens but had to retire through injury; I tried but failed to get Falkirk's Darren Barr, Darren O'Dea of Celtic and Sunderland's Russell Anderson and in the end signed Bob Malcolm, who'd returned from Australian football."

"We'd begun to struggle for goals and although Gary Harkins was getting plenty from midfield, we missed Higgins who was good at holding the ball up and making the play. Clarke, who'd previously done well at Clyde, was a disappointment, and that left us overly dependent on McMenamin and young Griffiths. We again made enquiries about Stephen Dobbie but he went on loan to Blackpool; we were turned down by Chris McGuire and Michael Paton of Aberdeen before we got Ben Hutchison on loan from Celtic, but that didn't work particularly well. Maybe if the board had invested £200,000 or so to sign Adam Rooney, who bagged 24 league goals for Caley Thistle - or had paid Dobbie's wages to get him on loan, we'd have gone up and I'd still be in a job!"

Even now, fans debate the decision to replace the experienced Scott at such a crucial stage of the season, especially when it appeared there was not the means - unless promoted - to pay for replacements. It is not uncommon for a new boss to turn things around at a struggling team, but far less so for a club to sack a manager while top of the league and expect his successor to guarantee title success. It was true though that Scott himself had replaced John McCormack in 1998, while Simon Stainrod had supplanted Iain Munro in 1992 - and both had gone on to win the league. But if the Scott sacking was not an error of judgement, had the board erred in bringing in Dodds - who had no managerial experience - rather than retaining the tried and tested partnership of Chisholm and Brannigan?

"It hurt to see Dundee going backwards on the park and when I heard the club had gone into administration my first reaction was not one of shock - nothing really surprised me after all I had experienced - but sadness. Management, office workers and players at Dens all worked well together and a lot of good people lost their jobs through no fault of their own. For a good while it looked touch and go whether the club would survive and although aggrieved at my own treatment, I was obviously pleased that things worked out - it would have been a tragedy otherwise."

"Later, Ray Farningham and I took the club to a tribunal for unfair dismissal. "We had nothing against Dundee but I felt it was a stonewall case of unfair dismissal. Calum Melville was unable to attend the original tribunal due to ill health and by the time of the re-arranged hearing, the club were in administration and consequently we received very little," revealed Scott.

"Dundee Football Club has always been my club and no matter the setbacks I encountered during my times at Dens I still stand by them. You don't spend a big chunk of your working life at one place and not have an affinity for it; it's not the club that sells you or sacks you, it's the directors who do the dirty deed and it's them I'm angry with. It really annoys me when people who know nothing about football make footballing decisions. Even when I was at other clubs, though, Dundee's result was always the first result I looked for, and it still is."

The Albion

So **what** did the future hold now for Jocky Scott? "It was going to be harder than ever for me to get back into the game again after being sacked by Dundee when the club was top of the league. I felt my reputation had been unfairly damaged by that decision and found great difficulty even getting an interview thereafter. It was a depressing time," said Scott.

"Then out of the blue I received a phone call asking if I would be interested in taking charge of Stirling Albion. I replied that they already had a manager but would be interested if the situation changed. The following day I received a call from Paul Goodwin a director and spokesman of the Stirling Albion Supporters Trust which ran the club. We met and after a quick discussion I was given the job. By then it was the third week in January 2011, I had been out of the game for almost a year and although the appointment was only part-time, I couldn't wait to get started."

Stirling Albion were founded in 1945 after the town's previous senior football team, King's Park, folded seemingly due to bomb damage to their Forthbank ground earlier in the Second World War. Under local businessman Tom Fergusson - previously managing-director of King's Park - Albion played at the newly built Annfield Park in a leafy suburb of Stirling within a quarter of a mile of the town centre. And for much of the next two decades, they gained a reputation of being too good for the lower league but never quite good enough to establish themselves in the old 18-club Division One.

Like many smaller provincial clubs, Albion struggled after league reconstruction and with gates dwindling and bankruptcy looming in the early '80s, Annfield was sold to the local council and rented back. Later an Astroturf pitch was introduced to cut costs and maximise income but faced with the cost of upgrading a ground whose main stand had had to be demolished, the council opted for a new purpose-built stadium on the outskirts of the town. It was called Forthbank and was less than a mile from the old King's Park ground of the same name. Annfield, which occupied a prime site, was closed at the end of the 1992-93 season and later demolished to make way for a new housing development.

Managers included Tom Fergusson, who took charge for three spells between 1945 and 1960, Sammy Baird, Willie Mcfarlane, Bob Shankly and Alex Smith, for 12 years from 1974 until 1986, George Peebles, John Brogan, Kevin Drinkell and Allan Moore. Matt McPhee, with 500-plus appearances, played most games, Billy Steele was their record goal-scorer with 129 goals, while other favourites to wear the red and white included

Henry Hall, Eric Schaedler, Brian Grant and John Brogan as well former Celtic, Hearts, Millwall and Sunderland striker John Colquhoun.

Things got no easier for Albion who fell out of the First Division in 1998 and after three years in the Second, slipped down to the Third from 2001 to 2004 until Allan Moore guided them back up. A further promotion to the First Division followed in 2007 and although Stirling - the only part-time team in that league - were immediately relegated, Moore took them back up as champions in '09/10 before departing to manage Morton who were a full-time club. A new management team of Moore's assistant John O'Neill and coach Roddy Grant took over but it was an uphill struggle and when six straight league defeats culminated in a 6-1 thrashing at Partick Thistle, the pair were sacked.

However, as far as financial situations went, Jocky Scott had jumped from the frying pan into the fire! Over the past 14 months, outgoing chairman Peter McKenzie (84), who had been on the board for 25 years and was known locally as "Mr Stirling Albion", had met tax demands from HMRC totalling £89,000 to prevent the club going into liquidation. In July 2010, having more than played his part in their survival, he agreed to write off a £1.2 million loan due to him by Albion and sold his controlling interest to the newly-formed Stirling Albion Supporters Trust for £300,000. That was enough to clear all debts and provide him with some recompense but it would remain a rocky road for the cash-strapped Stirling outfit.

By the time of his arrival, Scott's remit was quite simply to steady the ship and try to prevent the club again making a quick-fire return to the Second Division. "I appointed John Blackley - who had previously managed Hibs and worked alongside Gordon Wallace at Dundee - as my assistant but although I believed we could survive the drop to the Second Division, I had no idea of the difficulties we would face," said Scott.

"It was obvious from day one that the existing squad wasn't good enough and we needed some fresh blood. However money was so tight that I couldn't even sign a player on loan. On one occasion I wanted to bring in an unattached player - Stuart Duff - who had extensive SPL experience. He could have played three games as a trialist and was prepared to turn out for nothing as long as he got expenses but even that situation appeared problematic for the club"

Due to postponements, Scott and Blackley's first game in charge did not take place until early February. That resulted in a 3-1 defeat to league leaders Raith Rovers at Forthbank with Ryan Borris netting the consolation goal. But although that meant Albion had not won since mid-October, a glimmer of hope remained. Three-and-a-half months earlier, Scott's previous club Dundee had been hit by a 25-point deduction imposed by the Scottish League after entering administration for the second time in seven years. And that punishment left them bottom, 23 points behind the Forthbank side who then lay in seventh place.

However, even after enforced redundancies and the recent sale of Leigh Griffiths to Wolves, the embattled Dark Blues remained a force and had bounced back with an impressive string of results. In contrast, Stirling Albion were toiling - by the end of the year the gap had shrunk to eight points and after Scott's first game as manager they actually trailed Dundee by two points. Albion, though, had three games in hand and their new boss had an early opportunity to rectify matters when his old charges came calling a fortnight later.

The Dens men were on the crest of a wave and the match attracted 1,990 fans, three-quarters of them from Tayside as Scott commented: "It may well be Dundee that we are playing but it is three points that are available just like any other team and that is what I want to achieve." With regular home keeper Callum Reidford injured, the teams lined up: *Stirling Albion - Christie; McDonald, Buist, Allison; Doyle, McHale, Aitken, Borris, Forsyth; Mullen, Smith. Subs. - Gibson, Stirling, Welsh. Dundee - Douglas; Irvine, McKeown, Weston, Lockwood; Riley, O'Donnell, Harkins, Forsyth; McCann; Higgins. Subs. - Stewart, Rennie, Bartlett.*

Irvine's dismissal on the hour left Dundee with 10 men but although Stirling battled bravely, they were unable to overcome a first-half headed goal by Sean Higgins. That result put the visitors seven points clear although Scott, who had received a warm welcome from the Dundee fans, saw signs of encouragement: "Rab Douglas had three or four excellent saves otherwise we might have got something. I see a big change from when I came in and as long as we keep improving we'll give ourselves a chance."

Realistically, Cowdenbeath and Ross County, who lay just a few points above, were the sides Stirling Albion could catch. However, a disastrous five-day spell in early March saw just a single point taken from games against their nearest rivals. Derek Adams' side departed with a no-scoring draw then came a calamitous capitulation to Cowdenbeath. "A Michael Mullen double and another by Sean Welsh put us into a seemingly impregnable 3-0 lead but then the roof caved in," said Scott.

"In 77 minutes they pulled one back, they got another from a penalty and then Scott Buist was sent off. After that, we just went to pieces and lost the equaliser a minute from the end before they made it 4-3 in time added on. It was devastating," said Scott. Those games were our big chance but we blew it and thereafter things slipped away. By then, we'd conceded 50 league goals and until you get that side of things right, you're fighting a losing battle."

Throughout that month and the next, Stirling continued to labour and with five games left their hopes of staying in the First Division hung by a thread as they met Dundee at Dens Park on Sunday, April 10th. The Forthbank side had failed to win any of their past 21 games, while Dundee had come off the back of a remarkable 23-game unbeaten run. But although Albion would not win this one either, they stunned their hosts when Mullen put them ahead and went on to earn a well-merited 1-1 draw.

For months, Dundee had augmented their wafer-thin squad with experienced trialists such as Neil McCann but with the deadline past and forced to dilute their team with youngsters, there had been an opportunity for Stirling Albion to capitalise. A late, thumping 20-yarder by midfielder Paul McHale - a victim of the Dens Park administration cull - had had Robert Douglas at full stretch but it was too little, too late with their failure to win confirming Albion's return to the Second Division.

Relegation was hard for Scott but what followed only further emphasised the problems he faced with a fans-owned club without cash: "The squad that went down wasn't mine and I wanted to start afresh, retaining a core of the better players and adding fresh faces to give us a chance of bouncing back up. We had Hearts striker Gordon Smith and Hibs midfielder Sean Welsh on loan but they were both recalled. I basically cleared the decks and offered new deals to just six of those out of contract. Reidford and Allison and later Borris re-signed but unfortunately others rejected the terms and moved on."

"The most disappointing aspect of it was that while our skipper, Ross Forsyth rejoined Allan Moore at Morton, three others signed for rival teams in the Second Division. Scott Buist went to Brechin City, while Paul McHale and ex-Motherwell full-back Martyn Corrigan joined Stenhousemuir in nearby Larbert. I had to accept that we couldn't even compete with the likes of Stenhousemuir who are a well-run little club. But with all due respect, I don't think anyone would class them as bigger than Stirling Albion. It was all down to finance."

Stirling Albion were the first and only Scottish Football League club to be 100% owned by a fans trust, the Stirling Albion Supporters Trust having been formed by various groups of fans concerned about the future ownership and viability of the club. Speaking to the *Stirling Observer*, Scott had said: "I suspect our budget will be one of the lowest in the division and the model the club has, with it being owned by the fans, means there is not a benefactor there to put money in to help. I knew the budget was going to be slashed and I'm fully aware of the situation. The supporters are in charge of the club and they have to run it. Any money raised through the trust would help."

To that end, the Forthbank club had come up with a unique initiative *"So You Think You're Good Enough?"* as a way of raising cash as well as discovering talent. £6,000 was raised after 30 players each paid £200 to play in a series of trial matches, hoping to impress the manager and earn a contract. "It wasn't a bad idea as the club got good money and we picked up a couple of decent players in goalkeeper Sam Filler (20), a student at Stirling University who'd been at Middlesbrough and Bradford City, and defender John Crawley (24), an ex-Motherwell youth player who had spent four years on a football scholarship in Las Vegas!"

Scott, meanwhile had scoured the free-transfer market before bolstering his squad with around 15 newcomers, including ex-Dundee United full-back Jamie McCunnie and former Hearts striker Graham Weir. "I'm looking forward to the challenge. It's too early to be setting targets but what appeals is working with the players and trying to make them better. We may have quite a few young players but the good thing is you can coach them, whereas sometimes the older pros have a few bad habits which are hard to change."

The previous season's winless drought had ended with a 3-2 final day triumph against Morton and the '11/12 campaign began brightly with wins over East Fife (h), 1-0 and Dumbarton (a) 5-1. Seven points were taken from their opening three games but, ever the realist, Scott recalled: "I wasn't kidding myself for I knew it was a false dawn and couldn't last. The team was a mixture of kids and guys who, to be honest, just weren't good enough."

"When you see things going wrong on a Saturday your first instinct is to have the players in on a Monday to sort things out but with the club being part-time that wasn't possible," said Scott. "It was Tuesday before I saw them and you had to balance tactical and shadow play with the need to maintain their fitness levels as well."

At the start of October, a home win over Brechin City, the 9/4 promotion favourites, kept Stirling Albion fourth but as autumn turned to winter, five successive defeats without a goal scored saw them tumble down the table. There was also an early exit from all three cup competitions, which meant a reduced income stream. And when Airdrie United departed from Forthbank with a 4-1 win to leave Albion anchored to the bottom on December 3rd, the club decided it was time for a change. Scott and Blackley had managed just five wins from 38 competitive fixtures and two days later they were sacked. That however paled into insignificance for Jocky Scott with the news that his mother who had been ill for some time, had passed away.

Albion defender Greig McDonald took charge on a temporary basis before the appointment was later made permanent. At the age of 29, that made him the youngest senior football manager in the UK but despite his efforts, cash-strapped Stirling Albion were to suffer their second successive relegation that April and the club remains in the Third Division to this day.

For Jocky Scott it was back to the golf course though it wasn't too long before he returned as a coach at Aberdeen at the behest of veteran Dons boss Craig Brown and his assistant Archie Knox in September 2012, both of whom Scott was well acquainted with from their time at Dens Park as well as from the coaching school at Largs. After starting his career at Rangers in 1959, Brown had been part of the illustrious Dundee championship-winning squad of 1961-62 and had been with the club for the first six months of the young Scott's career.

His playing career was blighted by a succession of knee injuries but he was to excel in coaching and football management. After impressing as Clyde boss he became assistant-manager of the Scotland international team under Andy Roxburgh and succeeded him as manager in 1993. After a creditable eight years he returned to club management, first with Preston North End, then Motherwell before joining the Dons in 2010.

Knox's career had seen him play for Forfar Athletic, St Mirren and Dundee United until 1976 before managerial stints at Montrose and Forfar led to his appointment as Aberdeen assistant-manager prior to his two-and-a-half years as Dundee boss. Thereafter, he was content to remain a highly influential number two at Aberdeen, Manchester United, Rangers, Everton, Millwall, Coventry, Livingston, Bolton Wanderers, Blackburn Rovers - for whom he was briefly caretaker manager - and Motherwell as well as two spells as assistant-manager to the Scotland international team, before returning to Pittodrie alongside Brown.

By then, the much-travelled Scott was 64 years old, and with Brown 72 and Knox 65, that meant that there was no shortage of footballing knowledge at Pittodrie. Essentially, the Dons could boast the most experienced and managerial and coaching team in British football, leading Jocky Scott to quip: "I know what Aberdeen is all about and I'll do whatever I can to help Craig and Archie. Maybe they felt they just might need a bit of added experience!"

His responsibilities now centred on the development of the younger members of the first-team squad but the arrival of new manager Derek McInnes the following spring was to mark the end of the road for Scott at Pittodrie. It was also to signal a new beginning for the Aberdonian, as after almost 50 years in the game, he turned his back on football to accept a management position with office-cleaning firm CSG in Dundee. And although dedicated to assist in building up his new firm, do not rule out a future return to the game for Jocky Scott. Jocky's journey has been a long and eventful one and may still have some distance to run!

Chapter 20

Thoughts of Jocky

Jocky Scott is one of a select few whose careers in football have spanned five decades or more. Others that spring to mind are Sir Alex Ferguson and Craig Brown, and with Archie Knox and Walter Smith not far behind, the Aberdonian is in fine company indeed! As a player, Jocky's journey took him from the obscurity of the Chelsea youth team back to Scotland's north-east, where he enjoyed a long and distinguished career at Dundee, then became an integral part of a successful Aberdeen side before ending his playing days at Dens Park.

In the late 1970s, he spent two glorious summers in the USA playing for Seattle Sounders against some of the world's greatest footballers. But, by then, Scott was no stranger to foreign parts as several years earlier he had made his full Scotland breakthrough in Denmark and Russia. In addition to several visits to England, his Dens Park career allowed him to experience an abundance of international travel, European ties and tour games taking him to the Republic of Ireland, Holland, Belgium, Switzerland, Denmark, West Germany, Italy, France, Portugal and Sweden as well as the USA, Australia, New Zealand and New Caledonia.

His coaching and managerial career involved lengthy periods at Dundee and Aberdeen as well as at Dunfermline, Arbroath, Hibernian, Dundee United, Notts County, Raith Rovers, Sunderland, Plymouth, Viborg FF and Stirling Albion. Thus, having worked at no fewer than 13 different clubs - in mainland Europe, south of the Border and Scotland - Scott, who also served as an employee of the Scottish Football Association, is clearly a man with a wealth of experience as well as an in-depth knowledge of the Scottish game and his opinion is well worthy of consideration.

Scott talks intelligently about how the game is played. He studies the shape of sides prior to kick-off, who their main playmakers are, whether they play with width and how often the long ball is used. He has an analytical mind and automatically checks if the opposition defence holds a high line without putting pressure on the ball. He checks defensive and attacking set-ups at all set-pieces and considers whether any individuals in the opposition have a suspect first touch, what their work rate and positional play is like. In short, his attention to detail is minute.

Professional football today is so different from when Jocky signed on the dotted line for Dundee in 1964, so how do things compare? "So much has changed and not all for the better," mused Scott. "Back then, there were just two top leagues in Scotland - Scottish League Division One and Division Two - and the whole philosophy of things was different. Nowadays, players are advised to eat healthily and a lot of time is spent on nutrition and preparation generally. Fitness and Sports Therapists and Physiotherapists guide players on fitness and rehabilitation from injuries while Sports Scientists are available to advise on diet to maximise their performance."

But although acknowledging that the approach to nutrition has greatly advanced, Scott was quick to add: "In the '60s and '70s, there were top-class Scotland internationals like Billy Bremner of Leeds United and Dave Mackay of Spurs and Derby, whose energy levels were way above some of those I see playing now. Davie Hay - Celtic and Chelsea - and Stevie Murray - Dundee, Aberdeen and Celtic - would also have run all day if required, while Gordon Wallace was another who expended huge levels of energy. They didn't have the benefit of the advice provided now and probably ate all the wrong things. But when I compare them to some of today's players I'm tempted to say that this diet thing is maybe not all it's cracked up to be!"

"When I started out, the set-up at Dundee was similar to most clubs with manager Bob Shankly leaving the fitness side of things to our trainer Sammy Kean whose training stints were legendary. His favourite involved players walking in groups around the perimeter of the Dens Park pitch while he stood in the centre. Dear old Sammy would then give a blast on his whistle and point at an area to which the players - no matter where they were - had to scamper as fast as their legs would carry them! Then there was pre-season training when we pounded the streets of Dundee with Sammy setting the pace on his bike! Since then, though, coaching has changed out of all recognition with an emphasis on touch and movement and tactical awareness encouraged by forward-thinking coaches."

"However, current financial restraints have meant the demise of the reserve team and I believe Scottish football has lost something that played a big part in improving my game. Back then, there was an official reserve league and when Dundee's first-team were away to Celtic on a Saturday afternoon, the reserves would play their second string at Dens. Most reserve teams had a scattering of experienced players with the balance consisting of younger lads keen to make their mark in the game. Those not in the big team would have a regular game to look forward to and the fare on offer was usually well worth watching."

"Bobby Wishart was a cultured half-back who had won Scottish League Championship medals at Aberdeen and Dundee and although a veteran by then he was a huge help to me. He used to shout: 'Don't make that run - I'll never get the ball to you if you go there. Stand still and I'll knock it in to your feet'. These situations constantly arose and it was playing alongside Bobby and other experienced guys like Shug Reid and Bobby Waddell that provided myself and the other youngsters with invaluable experience," concluded Scott.

The book's originator, Peter Caproni, who was a winger with Stirling Albion, agreed with Scott on the value of reserve games: "I remember being in direct opposition to full-backs of the quality of Dundee's Alex Hamilton, Davie Holt of Hearts and Billy Dickson of Kilmarnock, who were all full internationals. Sadly, the authorities decided to axe the reserve league, thus denying today's up-and-coming youngsters the experience Jocky refers to, and that has hampered their development."

"In our day, it wasn't such a huge step because although there was still a considerable gap, the standard of the reserve league was pretty good and was excellent preparation for the first-team," said Scott. Back then, there was rarely a tactical change from the bench and experienced pros would alter things on the pitch but that wouldn't happen today!" So what's best - coaching off the park by astute managers and coaches or "hands-on", on-field coaching by tried and tested professionals perhaps in the twilight of their careers?

"Probably a bit of both," thought Scott. "I learned loads from experienced pros I played with and against in my formative years but also benefited from the coaching methods of the more modern era. The likes of Bobby Seith, then John Prentice and Jim McLean - who were a huge influence - and later Archie Knox, moulded my thinking and improved me as a player while giving me a great grounding as a coach as well."

Players like Jocky Scott himself, however, fall into the "inspirational and entertaining" category and coaching should be tailored to allow that individuality to continue to thrive. Scott, with his head-down, dashing runs at opposing defences was a natural, with only one or two rough edges to be smoothed off. Unfortunately, all too few talented individuals - James McFadden, Aidan McGeady, Gary Mackay-Steven and Gary Harkins are some who tick the boxes - now come through the ranks, which is a sad indictment on the domestic game."

"Is refereeing any better today? I have my doubts. Players are now booked for very little and myself, Jimmy Johnstone and Charlie Cooke would have loved that degree of protection as many a defender marking us would have been sent off! Increasingly, the "suits" at FIFA seem to want football to become a non-contact sport - a big mistake in my view as well-timed tackles are a feature of the game."

"All those new rules are killing the sport. The offside law? Nobody knows what's happening nowadays - it really is a joke. How can you coach defenders when players seemingly in an offside position are deemed onside as play is in its second phase? Bob Shankly and Jim McLean would have burst a blood vessel!"

"And hard men? Don't make me laugh! There's few if any playing today that could have lived with men like Dundee's Hugh Reid and Bobby Cox, Jimmy Millar of Rangers, Buck McCarry at St Johnstone and ex-Clyde and

Stirling Albion full-back Jim Burns. In those days, defenders were defenders and players like Dunfermline's Roy Barry, John McNamee of Hibs, John Cushley at Celtic and Airdrie's Derek Whiteford would always let you know you were in a game. These guys were the real deal and would have run through a brick wall for the cause."

"Almost every club had skilful, entertaining players. Celtic had Jimmy Johnstone and Kenny Dalglish, Willie Henderson and Willie Johnston were at Rangers, Dunfermline had Alex Edwards, Kilmarnock boasted Davie Sneddon while Willie Hamilton was Edinburgh's equivalent - for both Hearts and Hibs - to Charlie Cooke at Dundee. Aberdeen had Jimmy Smith and Joe Harper while John Connolly and Henry Hall excelled for St Johnstone and these dazzling stars flourished alongside stalwarts who equally endeared themselves to the fans by their effort and commitment."

Jocky has his own thoughts on how to improve the game in Scotland: "The game is crying out for change and I'd like the government to assist clubs to get their own training facilities which would include an indoor pitch especially for coaching youngsters. Just how can you coach kids when you have to concentrate on keeping them moving to keep warm? I think we should consider playing from March until October as too many matches go ahead in freezing conditions which suits neither players nor supporters, who in many instances are asked to pay ridiculous prices."

"Then, somehow, we have to find a way to take the fear out of our game. The SPL is too tight, relegation is a constant worry and too many sides concentrate on not losing rather than trying to win a match. It's not the manager's fault, it's the system. Before the start of any season, 75% of the managers would tell you their first priority is to remain in the league."

"The recent merger between the SPL and the Scottish League and their proposed investment and play-offs should relieve some of the pressure on cash-strapped full-time clubs in the First Division. But most managers, players and fans are fed up seeing their team play each other four times a season and there's absolutely no doubt in my mind that the top league should be extended to 16 clubs - the minimum size as recommended by UEFA."

When Jocky Scott strutted his stuff in the '60s and '70s, the status of Scottish football was far higher than it is now. Those were the days when not only Celtic and Rangers but others like Dundee, Dunfermline and Kilmarnock graced the European scene by reaching the later stages of European tournaments. Domestically, the Parkhead side ruled the roost, although others had their moments in cup competition, with Aberdeen progressing from their 1976 League Cup success to become the dominant force in Scottish football by the early 1980s.

Throughout that period, young players came through in abundance and players like Scott got an early chance to prove themselves at the highest level. The Scotland international squad, too, was awash with talent and after a tale of misfortune throughout the 1960s, Scotland qualified for five successive World Cup Finals between 1974 and 1990, before doing so again eight years later. So what changed and where did it all go wrong?

Until 1975, there were 18 teams in the top division, which was reduced to a 10-team Premier League to eliminate "too many meaningless games" and allow the bigger clubs to get a larger slice of the financial cake. Up to that point, gates had been split 50/50 but, thereafter, clubs would retain their own home drawings - the greatest beneficiaries being the Old Firm whose attendances were far in excess of the others. Effectively, the rich would get richer and by 1986, having completed the modernisation of their ground after the lessons learned from the 1971 Ibrox disaster, Rangers began to flex their financial muscle. Initially, they signed many of the best British players and then started to outlay big money on talent from all around the globe.

Aberdeen then Celtic were blown away as Rangers proceeded to dominate the title race for nine years until 1997, though it remained an annual Old Firm procession thereafter. In an effort to maintain a challenge, other clubs also brought in increasing numbers of "foreign mercenaries" often to the detriment of young Scottish talent. In the early '90s, Celtic came near to bankruptcy and later smaller clubs like Clydebank, Airdrieonians and Gretna went to the wall. Partick Thistle and Falkirk too found themselves in financial difficulty, while Morton, Motherwell, Livingston, Dundee and, more recently, Rangers, Dunfermline and Hearts went into administration - the profligate Light Blues suffering the humiliation of liquidation before re-emerging as a new company.

"The game is in a mess and I'm not sure that sending Rangers - or indeed any of the other full-time clubs - down to the fourth tier is the answer. I see no reason for having four leagues - the bottom two could be Third Division (East) and Third Division (West) with play-offs for promotion. That would mean any full-time club punished for an insolvency event could bounce back quicker, which would be to the benefit of the game in Scotland. Another option is for the SPL to expand the league to 20 teams, perhaps for five years to allow ailing clubs to get themselves in order. I'm sure the likes of Sky and the various sponsors would be happier with that and the certainty of half-a-dozen local derbies, rather than a 12-team SPL possibly shorn of Rangers, Hearts, Dundee and Dunfermline - sporting integrity or otherwise!"

"A bigger league would mean more certainty for clubs and managers who could then reasonably plan ahead. And accepting that there are only around 24 clubs of any size in Scotland, any bigger team unfortunate enough to take the drop would probably bounce back reasonably quickly - which is not the case just now. Let's see the projected figures for all the options, look at any shortfall and then see how we can make it up."

"Maybe tweak it to 18 clubs, perhaps with three up and three down for added interest. The old-style League Cup sections could bring added games, possibly with Celtic and Rangers meeting to generate greater revenue, though alternatively they could sit out the earlier ties and come in at a later stage if they wished along with other teams in European competition. Where there's a will there's a way!"

"Unfortunately, the same greed and lack of foresight that saw the SPL lose a good slice of their Sky revenue a few years back still appears to exist today. I think some chairmen of clubs already in the SPL - they claim to need the gate receipts from the extra games against the Old Firm - don't want a bigger league as their income would be diluted. Pathetic really and it's holding our game back."

"England has a far greater population than Scotland and that along with the emergence of Sky TV and its massive sponsorship has allowed their Premiership clubs to attract big names from all over the world. There's a huge gulf between the wages they can pay compared to up here with even the Old Firm struggling to compete against medium-sized clubs in The Championship and others finding it hard going to match what is on offer from teams in League One."

"Whenever talented young Scots now emerge - like Jack Grimmer, Fraser Fyvie and Ryan Fraser at Aberdeen or Dundee United's Scott Allan - they are snapped up by English clubs before they are old enough to merit much of a transfer fee. That means Scottish football is denied the larger investment it so desperately requires to take the game forward and if you keep pulling up the roots, eventually you won't have a tree," concluded Scott.

At the peak of his career, Scott would have been on a wage of something like £150 /£200 per week basic and, although bonuses took him well above the average British working wage, he would by no means have been considered wealthy. Which begs the question - how much would Jocky Scott be worth today? Almost daily we read of players in England receiving astonishing wages in excess of £100,000 per week and there is little doubt that if Jocky were playing today, he would have retired a very rich man!

Looking back, the Aberdonian is the first to admit that his managerial career was not all plain sailing. Part-time football brought its problems, Scott felt he was accorded too little time at Easter Road, while there were altercations with unhappy fans at Dunfermline, Notts County and Dundee as well as disagreements with the board at Meadow Lane. However, at Aberdeen, Scott is not only fondly remembered as the hat-trick hero when the Dons crushed Rangers in the 1976 League Cup semi-final before going on to lift the trophy. He was also highly regarded for his part in the Pittodrie club's highly-successful managerial partnership with Alex Smith, his departure coinciding with a downturn in the club's fortunes.

Some 66 miles down the road, Jocky Scott is still revered as one of the shining stars of the oft underrated Dundee side of the early '70s - which might have done even better had it not been for the dominance of the men in green and white hoops from Glasgow's east end. Statistically, we find he began no fewer than 420 league and cup games for Dundee - a total bettered only by Doug Cowie and Bobby Cox - with an additional 57 appearances at Aberdeen. Throw in 39 games for Seattle plus another 26 substitute appearances in Scotland and the total figure well exceeds the 500 mark, proving that Scott had durability as well as star quality.

Moreover, Scott managed 154 goals in his 433 appearances at Dens Park - a highly credible average of around a goal every three games - leaving him just a few behind Archie Coats who scored many in lower league games, and fifteen behind the great Alan Gilzean, Dundee's all-time greatest goalscorer, who averaged an incredible goal every one and a half games! And at Pittodrie, Jocky again proved his worth in front of goal by maintaining a similar scoring rate to that at Dundee.

Inevitably, opinions will vary but his triple stint as the Dark Blues manager - a Dens Park record - stands up well to closer scrutiny. He boasted a highly respectable Premier League record of taking Dundee to sixth and seventh place between 1986 and 1988, then fifth - the club's highest top league placing in 25 years - and seventh from 1998 to 2000. When he returned to the club he loved in 2008, Scott's task was to repeat his feat of achieving promotion 10 years earlier. But although he built a good side and Dundee remained in pole position, a buoyant Inverness were rising fast. Scott was axed and financial meltdown followed when the club went into their second spell of administration several months later.

In May 1981, Scott's efforts as a Dundee player were rewarded by a Testimonial match at Dens Park against Aberdeen. The relatively low attendance of 4,000 was no reflection on his popularity - more that many remained at home to ensure they saw the highlights of the club's promotion-winning match against East Stirling the previous day. In his 25 years as player, coach and manager, Jocky Scott was to prove a fine servant indeed to the Dens Park club, and in 2009, he was selected alongside greats such as Billy Steel, Alan Gilzean and Doug Cowie as one of the first to be inducted into the Dundee FC Hall of Fame at the Invercarse Hotel in Dundee.

In 1963, Jocky Scott's move into the senior ranks, with Chelsea, was commemorated by a small plaque which hung alongside another for Ron Yeats of Dundee United and later Liverpool, with both given pride of place on a wall of the Aberdeen Lads Club pavilion at Woodside, Aberdeen. That old wooden clubhouse has long since gone but memories of the excitement which Scott the player brought to the Scottish game as well as his coaching and managerial experiences described in Jocky's Journey are an integral part of the fabric of Scottish footballing history and will continue to live on.

Chapter 21

Jocky's Dream Teams

Jocky Scott played with and against many great players, some of them world-class performers like Pele, George Best and Bobby Moore. The Aberdonian also managed some great teams with many excellent players and at the author's request and after considerable deliberation, Jocky got down to naming his various Dream Teams. This is what he came up with.

"A team from players I managed at Dundee, Aberdeen, Hibernian and Dunfermline (4-3-3): *Theo Snelders; Stewart McKimmie, Alex McLeish, Willie Miller, David Robertson; Paul Mason, Jim Bett and Robert Connor; Charlie Nicholas, (all Aberdeen), Tommy Coyne, (Dundee), Hans Gillhaus, (Aberdeen). Subs. - Douglas, Duffy, Brown, (all Dundee), and Wright, (Hibs/Dundee), O'Neill, (Hibs).*"

"As you'll see, most of them were part of the Dons double cup-winning sides of 1989-90 and that's the main reason I have to go for them, for not only were they top class players, they were proven winners. That's not to say that any of those not selected could not have slotted in to such a good side, for they were top-notch as well.

"A team from players I played alongside at Dundee (4-3-3): *Thomson Allan*: great temperament, good hands - made goalkeeping look easy; *Alex Hamilton*: very fast with great ability on the ball, *Iain Phillip*: composed defender - great reader of the game, *George Stewart*: dominant in the air - a defensive rock, *Bobby Cox*: small but tenacious - a real winner; *Andy Penman*: classy player with great shot, *Charlie Cooke*: two-footed, brilliant dribbler with goal threat; *Jim Steele*: strong and versatile - a fierce competitor; *John Duncan*: powerful runner, strong in the air and a lethal finisher, *Gordon Wallace*: good movement, a natural goalscorer and the best striker I played alongside in competitive games; *Alan Gilzean*: magnificent header of the ball, just as skilful on the deck and goal-scorer supreme - a true great."

"Again, most of this selection would have fitted seamlessly into the best sides in the land. Cooke, Steele, Duncan and Gilzean all went down to England and did very well. Gilzean was revered by the Tottenham Hotspur fans in much the same way as he had been by supporters at Dens Park. He was a legend at both clubs, did well for Scotland and it was a real honour for me to eventually wear that number 10 jersey he had worn for Dundee on a regular basis," said Scott.

"Charlie Cooke, too, proved a big hit down south and although he is best known for his mazy dribbling skills, he could take a goal and was always likely to produce that killer pass that would dissect even the best of defences."

"A team from players I coached or managed at Dundee (4-4-2): *Rab Douglas*: great presence, good hands - comfortable with shots and crosses; *Rab Shannon*: determined with a great attitude, *Jim Duffy*: excellent reader of the game and a great leader; *Barry Smith*: versatile, dependable defender and another good leader, *Tosh McKinlay*: classy and great going forward, *Javier Artero*: positive with great pace and energy; *Gavin Rae*: energetic box to box player with an eye for goal, *John Brown*: strong and always a goal threat. *Robert Connor*: great ability, good dribbler and passer; *Tommy Coyne*: good pace and ability, terrific goal-scorer, *Keith Wright*: strong runner and fine finisher."

"Only Rab Douglas and Gavin Rae - to Leicester City and Cardiff City, respectively, made it down to the English Leagues but these are precisely the type of players you would wish as the bulwark of your team - solid, top-class professionals with big Rab a guy most teams in the country would have loved to have had between the sticks," said Scott.

"International teams from players I played against (4-3-3): *Bobby Clark* (Scotland); *Carlos Alberto* (Brazil), *Tommy Smith* (England), *Franz Beckenbauer* (Germany), *Francisco Marinho* (Brazil); *George Best* (N. Ireland), *Johan Cruyff* (Holland), *Vladislav Bogicevic* (Yugoslavia); *Denis Law* (Scotland), *Giorgio Chinaglia* (Italy), *Pele* (Brazil)."

"Well, just look at some of the names there! Who could possibly forget Pele, who played in four World Cup Finals in 1958, 1962, 1966 and 1970, and whose skill, speed, athleticism and goalscoring ability deservedly earned him the title of the world's greatest player. Or the elegant Franz Beckenbauer striding effortlessly through opposing midfields; the twisting and turning of Dutch ace Johann Cruyff, the attacking verve of Brazilian full-back Carlos Alberto, not to mention my fellow Aberdonian Denis Law."

"What a player Law was - sharp, aggressive, quick feet and just deadly near goal. Tommy Smith of course was a tough-tackling midfielder, a real winner for Liverpool, while Aberdeen's Bobby Clark was Mr Reliable in goal and a real good guy as well."

"International teams from players I played alongside (4-3-3): *Thomson Allan*, (Scotland); *Mel Machin* (England), *Mike England*, (Wales), *Bobby Moore*, (England), *Bobby Cox*, (Scotland); *Andy Penman, Charlie Cooke, Jimmy Robertson; Alan Gilzean, Gordon Wallace, Joe Harper*, (all Scotland)."

"The combination of big Mike England and the unflappable Bobby Moore would be the basis of a great side and I would have no hesitation in placing Thomson Allan behind them. Others like Penman, Cooke and Gilzean just oozed class, while Harper was lethal in the box. And although Cox and Wallace never actually won international caps, I held them in the greatest esteem and believe they were both worthy of wearing the dark blue of Scotland."

Jocky Scott's Record

Playing Career

Club	Duration	Appearances	Goals
Chelsea	1963 - 1964	youth-team only	n/a
Dundee	1964 - 1975	394 + 8 substitute	150
	1977 - 1981	26 + 5 substitute	4
Aberdeen	1975 - 1977	57 +13 substitute	23
Seattle Sounders	1977 & 1978	39	9
Total		516 +26 as substitute	186

Playing Honours	Season	Club
Scottish League Cup (winner)	1973-74	Dundee
	1976-77	Aberdeen
Scottish League First Division (winner)	1978-79	Dundee
Inter-Cities Fairs Cup (semi-final)	1967-68	Dundee
Scottish League First Division (runners-up)	1980-81	Dundee
Scotland International (full caps)	1970-71	v Denmark
		v Russia
Scotland Schoolboys (Under-16s)	1962-63	v Ireland
		v Wales
		v England
Dundee FC Hall of Fame (year of induction)	2009	

Managerial & Coaching Honours	Season	Club	Post
Scottish League Cup (winners)	1989-90	Aberdeen	Co-manager
Scottish Cup (winners)	1989-90	Aberdeen	Co-manager
Scottish League First Division (winners)	1997-98	Dundee	Manager
Scottish League Alba Challenge Cup (winners)	2009-10	Dundee	Manager
Tennent's Sixes (winners)	1987-88	Dundee	Manager
English Premier Reserve League North (champions)	2003-04	Sunderland	Reserve-coach
Scottish Premier League (runners-up)	1988-89	Aberdeen	Co-manager
	1989-90	Aberdeen	Co-manager
	1990-91	Aberdeen	Co-manager
Scottish League Cup (runners-up)	1987-88	Aberdeen	Co-manager
	1991-92	Dunfermline	Manager
	1997-98	Dundee Utd	1st-team coach
Scottish League First Division (runners-up)	2009-10	Dundee	Manager

Jocky Scott's Record

Coaching and Managerial Timeline

Club	Duration	Post
Dundee	1980 (Jan) - 1986 (Jun)	Reserve-team coach, assistant-manager
	1986 (Jun) - 1988 (May)	Manager
Aberdeen	1988 (May) - 1991 (Sep)	Co-manager
Dunfermline Athletic	1991 (Sep) - 1993 (May)	Manager
Arbroath	1994 (Jan) - 1994 (Apr)	Manager
Hibernian	1994 (Aug) - 1996 (Dec)	Assistant-manager, interim manager
Dundee United	1997 (Sep) - 1998 (Feb)	First-team coach
Dundee	1998 (Feb) - 2000 (May)	Manager
Notts County	2000 (Jun) - 2001 (Oct)	Manager
Raith Rovers	2002 (Jan) - 2002 (May)	Manager
Sunderland	2002 (Nov) - 2004 (Nov)	Reserve-team coach
Plymouth Argyle	2004 (Nov) - 2005 (Sep)	Assistant Manager
Viborg FF	2006 (Aug) - 2006 (Dec)	Assistant head-coach
Scottish FA	2007 (Jul) - 2008 (Oct)	Youth Initiative Monitoring Officer
Dundee	2008 (Oct) - 2010 (Mar)	Manager
Stirling Albion	2011 (Jan) - 2011 (Dec)	Manager
Aberdeen	2012 (Oct) - 2013 (Apr)	First-team coach